AWAKEN

YOU ARE THE

ONE

Marelize Kloppers

Order this book online at www.trafford.com/08-0220
or email orders@trafford.com

Most Trafford titles are also available at major online book retailers.

Note for Librarians: A cataloguing record for this book is available from Library and Archives Canada at www.collectionscanada.ca/amicus/index-e.html

ISBN: 978-1-4251-7158-2

We at Trafford believe that it is the responsibility of us all, as both individuals and corporations, to make choices that are environmentally and socially sound. You, in turn, are supporting this responsible conduct each time you purchase a Trafford book, or make use of our publishing services. To find out how you are helping, please visit www.trafford.com/responsiblepublishing.html

Our mission is to efficiently provide the world's finest, most comprehensive book publishing service, enabling every author to experience success. To find out how to publish your book, your way, and have it available worldwide, visit us online at www.trafford.com/10510

www.trafford.com

North America & international
toll-free: 1 888 232 4444 (USA & Canada)
phone: 250 383 6864 • fax: 250 383 6804
email: info@trafford.com

The United Kingdom & Europe
phone: +44 (0)1865 722 113 • local rate: 0845 230 9601
facsimile: +44 (0)1865 722 868 • email: info.uk@trafford.com

10 9 8 7 6 5 4 3 2

This book is dedicated to my beautiful baby girl, Jayde who is my incarnated angel.

Thank you also to everyone who has played a part in my life for all the experiences I have ever had, have made me who I am today.

Most of all thank you to the great consciousness for giving us this experience to realize, once again who we truly are.

Contents

Introduction

You may be thinking if I am the one, what about everyone else who reads this book? The one for what anyway?

In your hands you are holding the potential to be the one. Being the one automatically entitles you to be everything you want to be and to have everything you wish for. Your greatest dream can become your reality as soon as you realize you are the one. The only secret is to know. Carry on reading and all the secrets and explanations will be given to you. You are now ready to know. Welcome!
Just the fact that you have this book in your hands means you are finally ready after a long journey of suffering, learning and searching to find out who you really are and what your purpose is. This is the beginning of the rest of your life!

This book brings philosophy, psychology, metaphysics, quantum physics and spirituality together. There are a lot of spiritual concepts that scientists are starting to prove, especially in quantum physics, but there is so much that science cannot even begin to grasp. Scientists now know that everything is made up of subatomic particles that have no mass but they cannot explain why something that is made up of mass less particles has mass. They also cannot explain what love is. According to science, it does not exist if it cannot be perceived by the senses and if it can, it is definitely, without a doubt, real.
This book attempts to explain why life is the way it is, why we experience it the way we do, what it really is all about and what we can do to make the best of it.

For all eternity the human race's biggest question and quest has been to find out what is beyond the sky and why we are here. Everybody is asking everybody else but nobody knows. So every now and then somebody comes along and says 'I Know" and starts another religion. The

problem is that they do have some of the truth but mix it up with control and power and then the picture gets quite distorted. So what is the truth? The secret is to look at all religions and find the common thread that runs through all of them. You will find that the only common thread is love but a lot of fear gets thrown in between. By trapping people in fear, they gain a huge amount of power. By trapping someone in fear, one gets to be the hero who saves them from this fear and therefore can get them to do pretty much anything.
Love is the only thing that is real and where there is love; fear, grief, anger, resentment, poverty, suffering and all other negative negativities cannot exist. The problem is that it is very difficult to stay in the feeling of love and not to get sucked into the fear and other emotions that destroy our perspective of who we really are.

Think about what your life consists of. Is there a lot of fear? Anger? Stress? Worry? Poverty? Struggle?
How would you like to live a real life consisting of peace, harmony, love, joy, no stress and anything else you want? This is the life you are meant to live and you can make it happen.

This book by no means contains everything you need to know or that there is to know. I have dedicated my life to understanding the truth and this is my understanding of what I have found.
For a long time I delayed finishing this book because I always wondered when I would know everything and if everything I knew was complete. I would often have experiences that would teach me that everything I thought was the truth, was suddenly not or that there was much more to the picture. I wanted to have the whole truth before putting it down on something as permanent as a publication and did not want to regret having said something a year after publishing. I wanted to be sure of my facts.

I soon realized that we can never know everything, firstly because consciousness is ever expanding and secondly because our human brains are limited to not being able to picture and therefore not being able to understand everything. The human brain always needs a physical example to be able to grasp any concept. There are many concepts that go far beyond anything physical and therefore we have nothing physical to compare it to, to get a picture.

People are all at different levels of consciousness. The same person is also at different levels of consciousness at different times of his / her life. Things can be interpreted on many, many different levels. When reading this book you will interpret it at your own level but if you read it again in a while, you will find that some things have a completely different meaning when you go deeper into it and the bigger picture becomes even clearer. A year from now I might see things quite differently as to how I express them in these pages or I might realize that the way the topics fit together are even more complex.

This process of realization happens in the same way that a child learns about numbers and then learns that these numbers have relationships to one another and that they can be added, multiplied, divided and subtracted. He later learns that there are many, many other things one can do with numbers and eventually he will realize that we haven't even begun to start using numbers to their full potential and that the possibilities are endless.

It was also very difficult deciding what topic to start with because every concept is so intertwined with every other concept and you have to understand the one to understand the other. The concepts all web into each other and it is very difficult to try and explain it in a linear fashion so it is quite complicated to put the information in a sequence that flows from one topic into another. You may find that because of this there will be a bit of confusion and many questions may come into your mind

as you read. Don't worry about it, just carry on reading. Everything will be explained as you proceed.
I decided to start with emotions as this ensures that beliefs and fears don't hinder your ability to grasp the rest. Once we have that under control, we become open to receiving the truth. There are some very controversial statements in here but you will see that the truth can be recognized very easily and that some things are true whether you believe in them or not.

It would not only be unrealistic but also irresponsible of me if I were to say that reading this book will make all your problems disappear. What I can assure you though, is that if you follow these ways, you will see life in a new light and will find more appropriate ways in dealing with life, other people and your problems. You will also find yourself and discover a new sense of confidence and self worth.

This book is about what exactly is real and what is not real, who we are and who we are not, who God is and who he is not and most of all what is truth and what is illusion. This is the part in the matrix where you choose to take the red pill or the blue pill. This is the part where you choose if you want to know the truth and the whole truth or if you prefer being ignorant to it and denying the responsibility that comes with knowing. Once you know the truth, there is no going back. It is a huge step in your spiritual evolution with very rewarding effects. By the end of this book you will have all the secrets to make your best life possible. Congratulations for having come this far and good luck on the greatest adventure of your existence on earth!

Section 1

Know yourself

Active memories creating belief systems

The first step to becoming who you really are is to clean the windows you observe the world through. If they are covered with dirt, you cannot see clearly and get a distorted picture. Emotions, belief systems and active memories is the dirt that prevents us from seeing the full picture of life.

Belief systems are created from the moment we are born. With every single little thing that happens in our lives, we experience a certain emotion. This emotion either makes us feel positive or it makes us feel negative. Our minds then decide if it wants to experience that emotion again or not and then makes a rule or a trigger that warns us when we are in a similar situation. These triggers can come from any silly little experience and are completely on a subconscious level. They are decisions we make about life so that we can more or less predict what the outcome of a situation will be. This is a form of self-protection. It allows us to predict and avoid situations where we could get hurt. When these triggers work for us we turn them into a belief system. For example to protect yourself in traffic your mind may have decided that "I believe that all drivers are stupid". You will drive more carefully due to this belief but you will also judge every little thing someone does in an unforgivable way.
When these triggers kick into place it is called an active memory. This means that there is an emotion behind the situation that relates to a previous experience but does not necessarily have anything to do with this situation. An active memory is a memory with an emotion attached to it. Therefore you immediately judge this situation according to how the last situation was. For example: Your wedding turned into a divorce (active memory). I hate weddings (protective belief system).

Here are a few examples of how belief systems are created:

1) During your childhood your father was absent and you never experienced a close relationship with a male figure. This then leads you to subconsciously believe that men are not reliable, can't open up properly, you can't have a close relationship with a man, all men will abandon you, etc. As a result you avoid men and make a point of not getting close to them. Your active memory (the emotion that comes when thinking of your relationship with your father) automatically triggers a belief system (I cannot have a relationship with a man) whenever you start getting close to a man. This belief system can be so strong that even if you meet a man who is reliable, opens up and truly has potential to be close to you, you will drive him away because you will never believe that he is really honest, loves you and is close to you.
This is exactly how your worst fear becomes your reality. Your belief system can create the exact situation you are trying to protect yourself from. It prevents us from seeing clearly.

2) Your coworker stabs you in the back after thinking that he was a really nice, honest, reliable person. This then leads you to believe that you can't trust anyone, people are not as they seem, and everybody is out to get you. Your belief system makes you become defensive all the time and doesn't let anybody come too close to you so that you can protect yourself before they hurt you. As a result people will stay away from you and your beliefs are strengthened as people avoid you and defend themselves against you. Catch 22!

3) Your 2-year-old pulls the tablecloth and the entire Christmas dinner lands on the floor and your guests are due to be there in 10 minutes. You give him the hiding of his life and your stress levels just rocket off the scales. You then create a belief that Christmas is a hassle and you

start moaning how you are always the one having Christmas at your house and nobody else ever makes the effort. In turn, depending on how you handle the situation, your 2-year-old could learn that Christmas dinners are painful with lots of tension in the house and could even develop an allergy to the food served at that meal!

4) Your dad was very controlling and dominating when you were a child. You were never allowed to speak up for yourself, do what you wanted to do, or say what you really wanted to say. To cope as a child trapped in that world, you became either very strong inside and resistant to control or very cooperative in order to avoid conflict. Now as an adult everything you experience goes through that belief - I will not be controlled. So when someone tells you to do something; resentment, anger, hatred, self pity, depression, jealousy, and irritation kick in.

Belief systems can rule us all the time if we do not learn to recognize them. We need to learn to judge each situation for what it is, not from past experiences.
When we have a belief system, we expect something to be a certain way. For example: because some airplane crashed last week, you believe that flying is dangerous. Now you will never fly because your belief stops you. Belief systems limit us to live according to them. They also limit us from experiencing the varieties of life. Just because a certain situation turned out a certain way last time, does not mean it will be the same this time.

Not only does everybody have their own belief systems but they also adopt other people's beliefs. A child has very few beliefs but gradually accepts what his parents tell him as the truth, even though it may be based on their own beliefs. For example, a child eats a piece of food that just fell on the floor and the mother tells him if he does that he will get sick. Even though there may be some truth in it, it is still just a belief system not a fact. "You can't go out with no shoes on", "you must eat all the food on your plate", "don't talk religion or politics", and "you can't teach an old dog new tricks" are more examples of completely unjustified rules we have according to other people's beliefs.

Here are some more examples of common society belief systems that are not necessarily true:

Appearance is reality,
What you can perceive with your senses is what is real,
Everybody who is bigger than you, is more clever, more powerful, or stronger than you are.
Everything has limits,
Always consider what other people will say,
We are the only world that exists,
Every important, book, machine, object, etc has already been made,
Every person and every thing is all separate from each other,
You know nothing until someone teaches you,
If nobody can back you up, it is not true,
Good guys win, bad guys loose,
If you are good you go to heaven, bad you go to hell,
Death is the end of life,
Bad people deserve to die and good people don't.

Beliefs and expectations inevitably go together because when we believe something should or should not be done in a certain way, we expect it to be so. Therefore when our expectations are not met, we feel angry or fearful. What is it that makes us feel that way? Maybe we are disappointed that our beliefs might be wrong. This makes us feel vulnerable and unprotected, because we did after all create these belief systems to keep us safe. That is why we feel angry, stressed, or anxious when something does not work out the way we thought or believed it should.
For example: You believe that all people are honest, so when someone lies to you, you get very angry and worked up.

Here are some more examples of how beliefs create expectations:
People have died in cars (active memory) so cars are dangerous (belief system) = People should drive courteously,
Children cause you trouble when they are not controlled = children should be controlled,
Men work hard all day and women do nothing = the woman must make dinner and do the dishes,
I do my job properly so other people better do theirs properly = the mail must get here in time.

Another way to get us going is when something triggers an active memory and the fear of it happening again gets expressed as anger, violence, or fear.
For example: Last time the children didn't pick up their toys, you tripped and hurt your foot. Now you see toys all over the floor and you start screaming at the children to pick them up because you are scared that you might trip over them again.
This is how belief systems and active memories become little "buttons" that can be pushed to send you over the edge and once people catch on to what your buttons are, they will push them continuously just to get a reaction from you and subconsciously have power over you. If you refuse to let them push your buttons or rather not to react to it, they loose that power over you.
Even though it is inevitable to build belief systems throughout our lives, we must be aware of them and be careful not to let them restrict or limit us. It has become so normal and accepted in our society to live like this but always remember that just because restricting ourselves with rigid beliefs and mindsets is considered to be normal, does not mean it is beneficial or healthy in any way.
The more rigid your beliefs become and the more there are of them, the more likely it will be that you will be living from outburst to outburst. Your blood pressure goes up and your nervous system is a wreck. You will start feeling like a walking time bomb.

If your buttons are an explosion waiting to happen you can never be happy because your happiness is always conditional - you can only be happy if life goes the way you believe or expect it to go. This allows your beliefs to have total control over you. When something "goes wrong" (according to your beliefs), you might think, "I have every right to be angry" and blame it on external influences (the aspects of whatever the situation is). But, by thinking this, you are giving the narrow-minded part of yourself free reign to disempower you further and prevent you from moving on.

When you have so many buttons that other people become weary of you, it inhibits anyone from being themselves around you and prevents you from truly ever knowing someone and having a close relationship. This is just another way of protecting yourself. Some people believe so strongly that people will hurt them that subconsciously they will set people up to disappoint or hurt them just so that they can hold onto that belief!

A belief creates an opinion and opinions always need to be justified. There is a need to defend them. Remember that opinions are just based on memories and belief systems. Opinions always have an opposite, which can be justified just as much as yours can.
It's not what we don't know, that is holding us back, but rather what we think we do know, that does.

Beliefs also lead to rules, which makes us obey them, leading to a certain behaviour. In other words, if we believe ourselves to be stupid or incompetent, we may obey that rule and act it out.

You may be asking, "Ok, so what can I do about it?"
Firstly, just be conscious of it. The more you become conscious of it, the more you will start realizing that when something "goes wrong" you are just disappointed because of some belief you had.

If you want to be really honest with yourself and make a good effort of recognizing your belief systems, you need to make a list of your good points and your bad points. Then analyze what made you that way. Think carefully of what made you loving, what made you jealous, what made you short tempered, etc? That is a good way to find your active memories and belief systems. You will be helping yourself with constructive self-analysis, not self-criticism.

If someone irritates or makes you angry in some way, look at what they do that makes you feel that way. Then look at why that bothers you so much. It is normally something that you expect them to do or not to do because of your own belief systems. If someone is selfish and demands the world to revolve around him it may bother you because you would never do that. You may even be jealous that they have life so easy and you always have to work so hard for everything you want. Let it go and see it as their way of learning the lessons they need to learn in life.

When something upsets you, ask yourself at that moment, “Now, can I let go of my need to know this, to have this, to do this, or to avoid this?” Then ask “will I let go of it and when?” ”Will this matter a year from now?”

Don’t allow anyone to dictate your mood. That is letting them create your reality.

An interesting way of finding your reactions and link them to your beliefs is to do the following exercise:

Write on a piece of paper “I feel guilty when” 10 times leaving a line or two open under each one. Repeat for anger, frustration, sadness, fear, happiness, stress and any other emotions you want to. Then think about them and complete the sentence. Do as many as you can think of.

Now add “because” after each answer and think about what the belief is that makes you feel that way. Think about your beliefs carefully and consider if they are serving you or restricting you.

For example:
I feel guilty when I do something to upset someone **because** it is my responsibility to make everyone happy.
I feel angry when someone criticizes me **because** I am who I am and won't change for anyone.
I feel scared when I am not in control **because** if I am not in control, everything will fall apart.
I feel happy when I do something for someone **because** other people's happiness is more important than my own.

Another exercise one can do to get to the bottom of your belief systems is to analyze your memories. It has been proven that people remember those events from early childhood that are consistent with their present view of themselves and the world around them. In other words, we tend to remember things that confirm our core self beliefs. Therefore, if you analyze your most prominent memories, you can pinpoint the active memory and the belief system that is related to that.

When you stop living according to the restrictions you have created for yourself, your beliefs will start disproving themselves and you won't get so involved in the situation anymore. So for example: When your husband does not take out the trash, you will not start screaming at him. You will realize that you are just upset because you believed that he should and he didn't, so now you are disappointed. You will instead ask him nicely if he would be so kind as to take the trash out. Now don't expect him to say yes because of your belief that if you ask someone nicely they must do it!
Always remember that it has nothing to do with what the other person has or hasn't done. It has everything to do with your belief of what they should or should not have done!
Just watch how your relationships with all people change when you handle situations like this! Be careful though not to turn that into another expectation!

Another thing to be really careful of is not to replace exploding with imploding and suppressing the emotions. The trick is to not let things get to you, not to hide the fact that they are getting to you. Embrace life rather than resist it. If your belief systems define who you are but they are running you down, why hold on to them. Let them go! Why do you think you need to carry all this heavy baggage with you? Maybe you think the bags are a fixture to your hands. Imagine the relief when you find out that you can put them down!

We all make the mistake of blaming our lack of joy on the missing ingredients and the things we cannot change. This is a sure way of setting ourselves up for disappointment and constantly experiencing unhappiness. When our perspectives change, our environment will automatically change with it and happiness is an automatic by product.

Right and wrong

We have all been programmed to believe that certain things are right and certain things are wrong. Everything gets determined by that - how to bring up children, how to drive, who to be, where to live, and the list goes on. If you think about it, who gets to decide this? There seems to be so many standards. Some people's rights are other people's wrongs and vice versa. And then on top of that sometimes wrongs become rights and also vice versa. It seems to change every decade! Just 50 years ago it was a sin to dance and now it is so commonly accepted that there isn't even debate about it anymore. The same goes for showing sex and violence on TV. There are so many debates about this, I won't even begin.

Everything we believe is merely an opinion, a person's belief system according to some experience they had. Some person may believe that for example switching off a life support machine is completely wrong while another person believes it is completely right. The same goes for abortions, the death sentence, homosexuality, monogamy, corporal punishment and even things that most of us agree on like children should go to school, it is right to go to church, it is wrong to hit a woman, etc. Even though they are agreed upon, it still doesn't mean it is right or wrong. It is still just opinions. When we accept everything as it is, there is no reason to agree or disagree with anything.

We make sure everything in our lives have good or bad written on it in our memory box. This is another way of storing information to protect ourselves. It makes us feel safe from the unknown, from each other, from being judged, from getting hurt, and everything else that we are afraid of because we can either stay away from that situation or we can protect ourselves from it.

E.g. if you believe that going to prison is bad, you will protect yourself from it by avoiding it. Believing in right and wrong makes our environment so much safer. If everyone mutually decides what is good and what is bad, then we will know what to do to be accepted or rejected by society.

It also gives us an amazing sense of power and control. We can control people to do what we want them to do by telling them what is acceptable and what is not. We can also live in less fear if we are sure that people won't do anything unexpected or "wrong". The entire concept of right and wrong was basically designed out of fear. Fear of what other people are going to do and fear of being judged and rejected.

Therefore there is no such thing as right or wrong, there are merely actions (you do something) and consequences (something will happen). If you bump the table, the glass will fall over; when you say something, somebody will feel something; when you walk, the air moves, etc. When you do something, other people or events will change to suite the new environment. When one single atom moves all the other atoms around it also need to move to adjust to the new environment. Therefore whatever you do has a consequence. Essentially, however, there are no good choices or bad choices. All choices result in a specific experience and all experience brings knowledge and wisdom. Therefore all experience is good.

So even though nothing is right or wrong, we can determine what will befit us or hurt us by observing what is done in love, and what is not. Don't let your opinions of what love is supposed to be, come in the way! Also realize that everything is as it is because secret laws are at play in our lives and it all happens for a reason.

Emotions

One of the most difficult things to do as a human being is to look beyond all our emotional baggage. All these active memories and belief systems are emotional baggage. We carry them around in our minds in case we might need them to protect us. Unfortunately it makes us live from reaction to reaction and we never get to see a situation for what it really is. We need to live each moment as if it is the first time - with no judgment. How much more fun and free would life be without all the preconceived ideas, if we could experience everything as a child would, like you are seeing it for the first time?
We are responsible for our own inner space and pollution and can easily change with a bit of love, for yourself and for others. When we try to understand a situation, instead of pre deciding how it is, we will find that it is actually completely different to the way we thought.

Nobody can make us feel or do anything. Nobody can make you angry, jealous, etc. It is a choice. No matter what happens to you, you can always choose how to act. Be careful not to re-act (act as you did last time).
Nobody can do anything to you. There is no power in this world greater than the power within you. It only becomes greater if you make it so. Even in an act of violence done unto someone, it is their choice as to how to deal with it, they can choose to be the victim or they can choose to let it make them stronger.

Emotions and physical health

Not only is emotional baggage unpleasant in our lives and very painful but it is also extremely detrimental to our physical health. Whenever we hold onto an emotion like anger, guilt, bitterness, etc, our bodies look for somewhere to store it. Most disease is from emotional blockages. These emotions get stored in the cellular memory and certain emotions tend to sit in certain parts of the body. This is because certain parts of the body symbolize or carry the physical part of certain emotions. There is a chemical made in the hypothalamus gland (in the middle of your head) for every emotion we experience. Every cell has receptors for these chemicals and some cells have more receptors for certain chemicals or emotions. When these emotion chemicals enter the cells, chemical reactions happen and the cells change. This can create illness. That is why certain emotions affect certain areas of the body more than other areas.

Here are some examples of which emotions affect which areas:

Liver: Anger, bitterness, and resentment are mostly stored in the liver and gallbladder. Ever noticed how alcohol makes a lot of people violent or angry? People who are alcoholics, are often suppressing these kinds of emotions.

Lungs: Lung problems often have to do with grief, not being able to accept life, not wanting to let go, feeling unworthy of living. Smokers are often trying to suppress these emotions.

Joints: Joints support us physically and give us mobility so when there is some joint condition it often points to feeling unsupported, being rigid in our beliefs, not wanting to move, carrying a load that is too heavy for us, etc. Specific joints can also tell us a bit more about what the issue behind it is. A hand joint might have to do with wanting to be too independent. A shoulder might be telling you that you are carrying too many burdens. Problems with knees indicate fear or lack of support.

Kidneys: Kidneys are always based on a fear issue. It might be fear of loosing something, fear of getting old, or fear of anything basically. It is common to get kidney infections when going through a very tough emotional phase.

Heart: This usually has to do with love, sadness or lack of love. Somebody who has hardened their heart may suffer from arteriosclerosis (hardening of the arteries) while somebody who cares too much for everyone else and not

enough for themselves may get a weak heart that has been overworked.
Prostate or gynecological issues: These are often people who love too much. There is nothing wrong with that but the problem comes in when they resent the other person for not appreciating or reciprocating their love. These ones can also have to do with things like worthiness of being a parent or having issues with your parents.
Digestive problems: The digestive system is all about absorbing, eliminating and digesting. When we have problems in this area it often has to do with digesting life or a problem, being oversensitive (irritable bowel), holding onto something (constipation), absorbing new ideas or experiences (nutrition problems), rejecting something (vomiting, heartburn or diarrhea), or rejecting anything good for you or issues around self hatred (eating disorders).
Throat or thyroid problems: These are both in the throat area and are all about communication. If you have been taught not to express your feelings or cannot get your point across it may influence these areas. Also if you are not feeling listened to or cannot talk about something. Little children often get tonsillitis for this reason and women often get thyroid problems when they are feeling suppressed or frustrated.

When you understand what a specific part of the body does it is easy to relate it to what is going on in your life at the time and why that area has been affected. Even in the case of babies born with these problems it could be an inherited emotion or a past life emotion that has not been dealt with. I believe actual inherited illness is very rare, it is often a case of inherited beliefs and emotions, which get carried across in the cellular memory (coding in the DNA). In many cases you can overcome the condition if you can overcome the emotion or belief.

Your body is able to regenerate itself very quickly. Joints take about nine months to be completely new to what it was 9 months ago. Eyes only take two days. For this reason we should be completely healthy and any illness or weakness should be gone pretty soon. But why is it that when you have an arthritis knee, it can stay like that for years? This is because of cellular memory. The emotion that is being stored in that knee is in the cellular memory and when it regenerates it uses that faulty coding in the DNA to make the new knee. Now if the coding of the DNA is wrong, how can we fix it? By simply working on the stuck emotion, we can release it from the DNA so that body part can be built new and properly.

Having baggage does not mean you have failed in some way. Now that you see your issues it is just an opportunity to release and heal them and realize that they are not who you really are. Release yourself.
There are various therapies that work specifically on this process including meditation, "the journey work", "Bodytalk", "NLP", "holographic repatterning" and "body alignment" but it can also be worked on, on an awareness level, where you are simply aware of and working on destroying all this baggage, so that you can be free.

Becoming aware of your emotional baggage

As mentioned earlier, emotions are a physical reaction. When you are scared, your adrenal glands secrete adrenaline, which makes you feel anxious, sweaty, out of breath and trembly. These symptoms are known as "fear". All emotions are purely physical and mental but the soul does not know what an emotion is. The soul only knows love. This is not the same as the "love" we experience from endorphins being released into our blood, we are talking about unconditional love here, which means it has no reason for being and no condition upon which it exists.

You cannot think straight or be yourself under the influence of stress, anger or worry because these are body feelings, not soul feelings. You have to relax, take a step back and then choose your response taking into consideration the feelings of the other person involved, whether your response has any effect (good / bad / at all) on the situation. If it is not going to change anything at all, why bother putting yourself through that.

Learning to control your moods and emotions is a very important thing to learn as it gives you insight into many situations and life becomes much easier and smoother.

To overcome emotions, right thinking needs to be practiced.

To find your "buttons", active memories or belief systems, you are going to have to be very aware of assessing a situation before reacting. This will take a lot of self-discipline and honesty within yourself. It is so easy to go back into old habits and patterns and react the way you used to. Therefore it is very important to keep observing yourself at all times.

The first step to understanding emotions is to observe them. Observe emotions in other people. Watch how they over react, get angry, feel sorry for themselves, etc and then see where you do the same thing.

Start noticing how you are feeling all the time. If you are feeling angry, acknowledge it. If you are feeling sad, say "I am feeling sad". This helps to separate the emotion from you so that you don't become it. Then feel it. Feel where in your body it sits. You can even give it a texture, colour and shape if you like.

Now look at why whatever happened, triggered you like it did. Start observing in yourself, what triggers your emotions. What other ways could you have reacted in? What makes you react in that specific way when there were at least ten other ways you could have acted? Realize that this opportunity was given to you to learn something about yourself and to find out what still needs to be worked on.

You can even ask the people closest to you to use a trigger word when you get caught up in your emotions. This word can be anything that will make you snap out of it but not increase your frustration. "Remember", "Belief" or "Love" are always good ones where "stop it" or "snap out of it" has the potential to make it worse. You will be amazed how these trigger words can pull you out of the emotion that was busy swallowing you just a minute ago.

Many emotions are caused by us doing something or being in a situation that we don't want to be doing or be in. This comes from not accepting that everything happens for a reason. We need to make a conscious decision that the situation we are in is exactly as it is supposed to be. This does not mean we cannot change it, it simply means we can relax and accept the process. We will discuss this in more detail later.

Masks and acceptance

Apart from active memories and belief systems running our lives, there is a common human fear of not being accepted to deal with, which also determines the way we do a lot of things. Many people are addicted to acceptance. This comes from one of the biggest human fears, the fear of being alone. We are so scared of being alone or rejected because we judge our self worth according to how other people see us. Being alone or rejected makes us believe that nobody loves us and that we are worthless. This fear may stem from childhood where we would die if we were left alone without our parents.

Because of this belief system, we will do anything to gain acceptance or fit in with everyone else. Therefore, every time we find something about ourselves that is not considered normal, we try to hide it. The more of these things we find about ourselves, the more we are suppressing our real selves. We create masks according to how we want to be seen.

When someone is proud of you or disappointed in you they have an expectation of you and you either lived up to it or not. Now you can see how ridiculous it is to try and make someone proud of you. Constantly seeking approval from others gives them enormous power over you. It may cause you to repeatedly put other's needs before your own and over compromise on everything. You only feel good about yourself when everyone agrees with you and no one criticizes or disapproves of you.

There are two ways to mask something about yourself that is not "accepted". The first way is to hide it with it's opposite. For example: Somebody tells you that you are too loud. To mask it, you may become super quiet instead and suppress your outgoing personality completely. The opposite can also happen where someone becomes over confident to hide a lack of confidence.
The other way to mask something is to exaggerate it to the extent where nobody thinks you are really like that, they think you are just being silly.
This may also happen if you are confused whether they were laughing at you or with you.
For example: You may become even louder after someone commented at you being so loud. You may take it that he liked it, so you feel accepted and become even louder.

To find your own masks, observe what qualities in other people irritate you and what you admire. You will probably hate someone who expresses an aspect of yourself that you feel the need to hide because if you have to hide it, so should they. You can either admire their courage to not hide that quality or you can be jealous of them. But then again, that could also just be their mask for something else.
Once you realize that most of the things behind your masks were only created because of other people's masks, you can release them and be free to be yourself again. People only judge other people according to their own issues. One person may love you being loud and outgoing, while others may have been told that they can't be like that, so neither can you. It is all about their own issues, it has very little to do with you.

People tend to wear the mask that they think will protect them the most from the harsh world. If they feel lost and vulnerable inside, they will wear a mask of strength. They may even strengthen their bodies to look the part. Instead they should not try to hide the vulnerability but explore it and rather find out what there is to be so afraid of. In doing so they will find that there is nothing to fear - like a child thinking there is a monster in the cupboard but when he goes to see if it is there, there is nothing.

You will find that the more you observe people, the more you will become aware of all their masks. Often we take on other people's masks in an attempt to connect with them. If one of your friends always plays the victim and complains about everything, you might join in on that to make conversation and be accepted by them. In another case one may take on someone else's masks to help them feel better. For example, if one feels ugly, the other will also pretend to be ugly to make them feel better. This actually doesn't serve them, it only helps them to keep their masks. Real help would be to show them the beauty in themselves instead.

Labels

From the moment we are born, we start collecting labels. Among our first ones are black or white, male or female. Later you will learn if you are labeled pretty or ugly, good or naughty, etc. Eventually we have so many labels that define us, it is difficult to see the real you beneath all of it. We have a label for the work we do, our social status, our knowledge, our education, our physical appearance, our social abilities, relationships, personal and family history, belief systems, politics, race, religion, and many more.

Labels are created as another method of protecting ourselves. We put everything into categories so that our belief systems can kick in as soon as we realize what category someone or something is in. Once you have placed someone in, for example, the category of gay or straight, Jewish or catholic, lawyer or doctor, etc, your beliefs on that subject will kick in and you will have a preconceived idea of what that person is like. The problem with this is that it is often completely wrong, as we have learned about belief systems.

Labels also give us a feeling that we belong. If someone says we are "cool", we feel accepted and loved. Often people will be something they are not just to gain a specific label. They want people to see them in a certain way. This is letting others control who you are. Being yourself, you need to be without labels. You don't have to be black or white, male or female, rich or poor, etc. Why is that of any relevance? You can just be you.

We limit ourselves by using labels. A good example is by labeling yourself "old". According to the different people's opinions what old is can really differ. If you ask a 5-year-old he will tell you that being 20 is old. If you ask a teenager, 30 is old and if you ask a 60 year old, 80 is old. You are just you. Why should an age define you? The soul is never old, it is eternally young.
All words only mean what they mean to us.
You have not failed unless you name it failed. You are not sick unless you say you are. You are not any label. It is all just manmade judgments and there is not even a standard for it. Labels are all based on opinions, which are based on active memories and belief systems.

Pay offs

Pay offs are something that we gain from doing something. In every situation that someone claims to not want to be in but does nothing to get out of, there is a pay off. The same applies for emotions we are holding onto. If we didn't want them there, they would be gone long ago, therefore there must be a pay off. If you can't control your emotional state, it means you are addicted to those emotions. There is a need to feel that emotion for some reason.

Here is an example of the pay off one gets from being angry all the time:

Being angry all the time is easier than trying to be nice all the time. You are in constant defense mode and nobody can hurt you. You never have to be nice or feel anything apart from your anger. If you stay angry long enough you convince yourself that nobody cares about you. That makes you independent and you don't need anyone anymore.

For example: a child with an absent parent. The child will long for a parent that has left until he or she comes to a point where they realize that, that person doesn't care about them. They will then take on the attitude of "if you don't care about me, I won't care about you". Deciding this they can finally stop the waiting for the person to return but take on anger instead of longing.

At a moment of anger, you feel no love so you don't want to be with the person you are angry at. Therefore if you are angry all the time you won't miss someone anymore, and your payoff is to be completely independent. Just a pity you are so dependent on the anger to mask your pain.

Anger gives you a lot of power because by being angry you can control everything and everyone and make sure everything goes your way. This makes you feel safe. Everyone will do as you say to prevent you from acting in anger and them being in your way.

Here is an example of the pay off one gets from being extremely overweight to the extent that you cannot move:

You can tell everybody that you have tried everything and nothing works, so they accept you and also feel sorry for you.

You don't have to do anything, everyone will do it for you.

There are no expectations for you to lose weight.

You can tell everyone how difficult it is.

Everyday is the same (since you have limited yourself so much) so you have that security of nothing unexpected happening.

It gives you a sense of being bigger and stronger. This need is often as a result of some form of abuse.

It keeps the opposite sex away from you. Another result of abuse, most often sexual abuse.

Payoff for helping people at your own expense:
Many people seem to be so generous and always go to the end of the earth to help other people. Not only does this give them tremendous self worth (because it makes them feel they have a purpose), it also makes them feel powerful when they can help other people. They have the power to make someone happy, change their lives and be the hero. This power can become quite addictive. Even though you feel you need to help everyone, you are not doing either of you a favor. You are interfering with other people's lessons and could be disempowering them by making them dependant on you.

If there is something you are struggling to let go of, search for what your pay off might be. You'll have to be very honest with yourself to recognize or admit what it is. Just remember that once you admit it, it doesn't have to be a part of you anymore, you can now let it go.

Other people's baggage that influences you

If you've ever walked into a room full of miserable people, you will know that unhappiness spreads more easily than any physical disease.
Sometimes people are so stuck in their issues that it is difficult to be around them and not get sucked into it. Remember that you always have a choice on your own reaction. You cannot always control other people's choices but you can definitely control how you want it to influence you. Don't be hurt by other people's choices; that would be choosing to be involved. Rather remove yourself from it if you don't like it. It may be difficult to absorb but there is no such thing as a victim. You can always choose how you want to be affected by something that has happened "against you". You can either remove yourself from the situation or you can remove your emotional involvement from the situation. I am by no means saying that we

should avoid emotions, just that we have a choice on how to use the experience. You are only a victim if you decide you are.

You could always use the situation to make you stronger, not to make you weaker.

You always have a choice, even the choice to be powerless and pretend that you didn't have a choice.

You may not be able to change your experiences but you can change your beliefs and then your experiences or perception of your experiences will automatically change with that.

Remember also that life places you at a point of "rotten choices only" when you are about to make a major breakthrough in your experience of who you are. "Bad" experiences help us grow and without them we would take much longer to learn what we need to. When you are facing tough choices, it is always an announcement from your soul to your body that your entire being is taking a leap forward. You are shifting into a whole new experience. Turning a page. This is always difficult in the beginning but if you stay positive, you will see how far you have come and how much better things are now than they ever were.

You don't get many of these choices in a lifetime so actually enjoy them because they are huge leaps in lessons. You cannot change your past but you can change the effect it had on you. Every end is just a new beginning.

People who hurt us

When you start observing other people's emotions you will notice that the difficult ones are actually just in a lot of pain. They are just acting out of fear, insecurity, lack of love, etc. If you just spend a little time asking them about their pain, you will find there is a little lonely child in every person that is crying for someone to just see their pain. Even serial killers, rapists, angry and violent people all do what they do out of pain. They all have their own demons that they are dealing with. Anger is a painful emotion.

Don't frown upon or be fearful of angry people, rather see the pain in what they are feeling.
We must realize that all attack is a call for help. You can even ask, "What hurts you so much that you feel you have to hurt me to heal it?"
When someone has hurt you, you can (a) defend, (b) attack, or (c) find out what they thought their good reason for hurting you was. This will help you see it from their point of view. It is very important to observe your reactions in a situation more than observing the situation that made you react. Always consider how someone else is feeling before you react. If you really understood where they are coming from, without you're opinions, you will probably react very differently. You will act, not react. Re-acting is repeating a previous act, and is based on a previous situation.
Obviously there are some people that are dangerous and are a physical threat to us. Just remember that their souls are good, they are just lost, confused and stuck in their own baggage and learning their own lessons.

Here is an example:
People that go around bullying other people are so afraid of being bullied themselves that they would rather put someone down to make sure other people know there is someone else who is the scapegoat. In this way he seems stronger and can hide from appearing weak. The alternative to this is that he becomes the bully because he is so angry about being bullied by others and believes that nobody can understand what he went through. So he will then make a point of making someone else feel his pain so that they can actually sympathize with him.
The bully's philosophy is "As long as you show everybody who the victim is, you are safe not to become it". This is the same for any type of abusive personality. They all feel weak and insecure inside.

Reading character

When you start understanding how emotions work, it becomes easy to read people's characters, thereby making it easier to know who to trust, or not to trust, who to go into business with and who not to, etc.

By studying other people's characters you can find their issues in yourself and be given an opportunity to better yourself and grow from it. When you start observing people you can easily see what their belief systems are and if you look deep enough, you can often see what active memory it comes from.

You will start understanding why a certain person is so aggressive and will be able to relate to them better. You will be able to connect better with the stuck up person as you realize they are just insecure. You will be able to encourage people to overcome their obstacles by focusing on why they have them.

This does not mean you need to go around counseling everyone. Reading other people's characters needs to be done in a very discreet way. Don't offer your observations to anyone unless it will be constructive. Making them feel judged and exposed will only make them angry and will not help anyone.

When we read character, it should never be done out of judgment, but merely out of observation. Always have a detached observation. In judging there are emotions involved. In observation there is none.

As an observer you just witness the laws of the universe at play.

We need to just love everybody for who they are.

Happiness

We've all heard the saying "happiness comes from within, not from without".
Most people seek external objects to make them happy. They are looking for happiness in the future and blaming the past for not having it. They believe that in the future they will have a certain material possession that will make them happy. They believe that when I have that bike, that house, that toy, that partner, then I will be happy.
When your happiness is determined by what you have, that makes it conditional. Happiness comes from within. It is the love you project and feel in all things. It is living on the path of love and gratitude.
Life is not about being happy some day in the future, it is about being happy now. What do you need to do to be happy now? When was the last time you changed something in your life?
The real measure of success is happiness, in whatever position you are in. When you see the good in every situation, you will always be happy.

If you are a workaholic, always working to be successful, are you happy? You have no holidays, no family time, etc. Does that make you happy? Is your success measured by how busy you are and how much money you have or it is measured by how happy you are in all aspects of your life?
When one is so busy all the time, a lot of adrenaline is produced, which one can easily become dependant on and confuse with happiness. One gets so used to adrenaline being pumped through your veins that you feel tired and lifeless without it and then it becomes easy to fall into depression. It is important to realize the difference between physical happiness (endorphins and adrenaline) and real happiness.

It is important that your life is balanced. Your happiness must come out in every aspect of your life, not just in work or just in pleasure. You must be happy in every thing that you do.

It is easy to think we have to live a certain way because we have no choice, but it is better to make a change instead of waiting in unhappiness and never feeling happy. No matter what choice you make, there will always be a lesson in it.

Not accepting the choices we have made in the past results in pain and suffering. We never like to take responsibility for our position and like to believe that something should have been different to how it was. What has happened, has happened and the only thing you can change about it is the way you let it depict your future. Everything happens exactly as it should have. It is all part of the bigger picture. We must remember that we always have a choice about our future. You can either let the baggage pull you down or you can stand on it to make you higher. People who make a different choice are people who change the world. The only thing constant in life is change. So instead of making everything a problem, deal with it and accept it.

Acceptance is a difficult thing to learn but a very necessary part of experiencing happiness.

We need to learn to become resilient. When life gives us a knock, we need to get back up quickly and positively. Success and happiness are determined not so much by what happens to us but rather by how we respond to it.

Quantum physics tells us that every frequency has a sound and that two sounds that are opposite in frequency can cancel each other out. They have proven this by canceling out the sound of a telephone and of cars with their opposite frequencies.

Emotions are also frequencies and by emitting the opposite frequency, you can cancel the negative emotion out.

When you feel hate, think of gratitude, see something good in what you hate. When you feel anger think of kindness - how can you help the person you are angry at,

not to make you angry again. When you feel fear, think of courage. Think of how your soul is eternal and how you have nothing to fear. When you feel anxious, think of something that gives you peace of mind. When you feel pressure, worry or stress, concentrate on being in the present moment and not in the past or future.
Gratitude is the most important way of being and it cancels out most negative emotions.

A Japanese scientist, Masaru Emoto has found that we can change water with our attitudes, emotions and projected energies. If everyone had to grasp the concept of this, the world would change dramatically.
His experiments reveal that when you expose water to love and gratitude it makes beautiful crystals but when you say something ugly like "you fool" to the water it makes no crystals. He continued to prove that all good things made crystals and all "bad things" prevented the water from crystallizing. Have a look at his book for the whole picture - "The hidden messages in water". It's truly amazing!
Since we are 70% water you can see how we can create our own reality. You just need to think it to create it. If you are positive and live in love and gratitude, you will become a beautiful crystal and when you are depressed, angry and if you think badly of yourself, you will never reach your true potential. When you are beautiful within, you become beautiful without.
These findings have tremendous value. This is the key to physically proving that we create our own reality, that love and gratitude is the way and that negativity is the illusion (it won't even form crystals).
Water crystals show us in a very physical, undeniable way that positivity creates and negativity destroys. When we are filled with love and gratitude we become crystals.

The entire purpose of seeking the truth is to find happiness because happiness is love and love is not an emotion, but rather the feeling of being who you are.

Being yourself

We are not only encouraged to be individual, we are expected to be but how do we know who we really are? There are so many personalities to choose from yet society suggests that we only have one true self somewhere buried deep inside ourselves and we are expected to somehow know what that is.
Society uses labels to describe different personalities. You can be loud, quiet, rich, poor, emotional, brave, funny, serious, withdrawn, etc. Do you really want to be known by a label that you have to try and live up to? If you are the funny one, you are always expected to be the funny one no matter what you feel like on any given day. It's hard work having to live up to your personality.

Everything is about perceptions. Everybody perceives everything around them differently based on their own beliefs, fears, labels, masks, etc. Some people will notice things others don't. Some people will always see the negative and others will always see the positive. We create an "I am" I'mage or I'mpression according to how we want to be perceived. I'm pretty, or I'm rich are some examples.

This is not your real self. Being yourself is not about being something someone wants you to be or trying to fit into any specific group.
It also doesn't mean you get to be as full of nonsense as you like and everybody else must just put up with it because "at least you are being yourself". "Being yourself" should be your real self, striving to be the best you can be. We have also discovered that even though everybody has a past, you don't have to define yourself by that either. It's not about "what happened" but rather on gaining perspective on "what is happening".

The discovery of who you are is an exiting but challenging quest. Only the bravest will find themselves. It is about

finding your purest self without all the baggage, belief systems and society expectations.
When you are truly yourself, there is no fear, no emotional baggage, nothing to hold you back. You can be the person that comes naturally to you with freedom from all limitations. How would you be if you were completely free in every aspect of the word? That is your real self. Love yourself by allowing yourself to be your real self.
You are a beautiful, unique human being and only you can be you, nobody else can fill your role and be just the way you are. The beauty of you as the individual is that you can be individual. You being yourself is your uniqueness. It is you being the piece of the universe's puzzle that you need to be. If you are not you, you will not fit. The universe is not complete without you! Therefore just be yourself. Nobody has anything quite like you have. You should be proud of yourself. Nobody can be like you, so don't try to be like anybody else, you can't. Just be yourself.

How do I discover who I really am?

Once you have been working on letting go of all belief systems, labels and masks, you might end up wondering who you are without all that. What is left?
The idea is not to be numb of all emotions or to deny that we have them. We are still human beings and part of the experience is to feel emotions, wear masks, interact with people, and live our lives everyday. The idea is to know when we are acting inappropriately and also to gain a good understanding as to what we value, where our boundaries lie, and what kind of relationships do or don't benefit us.

Values

It is vitally important to know what your values are in life in order to live a happy, satisfying life. A lot of unhappiness can occur if you are not living according to your values even if you don't consciously know what they are. Here is a little questionnaire to help you discover what they are. Do yourself a favour and take the time to do this properly. You will learn so much about yourself.

Think of 3 moments where you felt happiest. Why?
Example: When I was traveling because I felt alive.
So I value: Adventure and new experiences.
1)____
____
So I value: ____________________________________
2) ____
____
So I value: ____________________________________
3) ____
____
So I value: ____________________________________

Think of 3 moments where you felt overlooked and rejected. Why did it make you feel that way? Your answers should directly oppose your true values. E.g. you may have felt suppressed so your core value is freedom.
1) ____
So I value: ____________________________________
2) ____
So I value: ____________________________________
3) ____
So I value: ____________________________________

List 3 things that make you very unhappy:
1) ____
So I value: ____________________________________
2) ____
So I value: ____________________________________
3) ____
So I value: ____________________________________

List 5 people you admire most. Why?
____________________ Why? ____________________________
____________________ Why? ____________________________
____________________ Why? ____________________________

____________________ Why? ______________________________
____________________ Why? ______________________________

What are your top 10 values in life? Go according to the above findings.

Love	Marriage	Respect
Security	Power	Achievements
Health	Passion	Loyalty
Acceptance	Happiness	Integrity
Humor	Children / Family	Success
Kindness	Adventure	Freedom
Independence	Travel	Trust
Excitement	Honesty	Compassion
Intimacy	Integrity	Validation
Good communication	Freedom of expression	
Self worth	Confidence	Control
Being right	People	Other_______

What has happened in your life to make these your top values? E.g. you may value security because you were never in one place and was always moving around while growing up.

____
____
____
____
____

Which 5 emotions you would most like to avoid:
The opposite of your worst emotions will often point to your top values.

Rejection	Anger	Frustration
Loneliness	Depression	Failure
Humiliation	Guilt	Abandonment
Fear	Boredom	Other _______

Life Evaluation

Now let's evaluate your life.
Life balance test:
On a scale of 1 to 10, rate how happy you are with each area of your life with 1 being not so good and 10 being very good. Why?

Career__________ Why? ______________________________
Family and friends _________ Why? ___________________
Health________ Why? _________________________________
Money ___________ Why? ____________________________
Significant other _________ Why? ____________________
Personal growth _________ Why? _____________________
Fun and recreation ________ Why? ___________________
Physical environment _________ Why? _________________

What do you need to do to increase your life satisfaction?
____
____

What are your goals in life?:
Short term: ____________________________________
____
Long term: _____________________________________
____

How do your goals conflict with your values?
E.g. if your value is integrity but one of your goals is money, working for a large multinational company probably won't make you happy.
____
____
____

Where in your life are you are honoring your values?
____
____
____

Where in your life are you not honoring your values?

What you need to do to incorporate your values into your life?

What's your biggest regret if anything?

What would be your biggest regret if you suddenly found you had 1 week to live?

Who are you?

What 4 words do you think describe you best?

What drives you? Fear, desire, ambition, money, guilt, duty, etc.

When or where are you most happiest? Why?

If you could change one thing about yourself what would it be? --

How do you deal with stress and what makes you feel relaxed?

____

____

____

How do you think other people perceive you when they first meet you?

____

____

How do you think your friends perceive you and why are they your friends?

____

____

What do people value most about you?

____

What do you look for in a friend? I.e. what does someone have to offer you in order for you to be their friend? Is it acceptance, money, fun, loyalty, common ground, someone whom you can share problems with, etc

____

____

What is the most interesting thing about you?

____

What role do you normally play in relationships?

____

What do you believe makes one a good person?

____

____

What do you believe makes one a bad person?

____

____

Do you ever pretend to be something you are not to hide a weakness you don't want people to see? Explain.

Write down everything that makes you unique and special:
As a person ------------------------------------
At play --
At work ---

What are you really good at?

What have you been praised for?

Your job

It is a popular practice to let ourselves be defined by what we do for a living yet so many people hate their jobs. It's not about what we do for a living, but rather about what we do with our lives and this especially must be something that expresses who we are.

Therefore, the first step to finding your true self and making life easier, is to find something you can enjoy doing for financial support. (It does not have to be work).

What do you love to do? When in your life have you felt completely at peace and full of joy? Was it when you were sitting in the mountains, looking after a child, working in the garden, organizing things, being creative, helping others, etc? List three or more things in the duration of your life that you have really enjoyed doing and then analyze what kind of work will be expressing your true self the most? What can you do that you will really enjoy and it won't even feel like work? If you want to do nothing and read books in the mountains, then find something that can support that lifestyle. It can be done!

You have to be yourself for a living to attain happiness. If you care about everyone and love animals then become a pet policeman. If you love cleaning, be a cleaner. If you love protecting people, be a lawyer. If you are good at organizing and enjoy working with people, be a manager. It is so simple to fall into the trap of just getting a job for the sake of getting a job and paying the rent when you could be doing something you love. To find out who you are, think of all times big or small that made you feel truly happy or at peace. A feeling of aliveness.

Your image

Just because you are now being yourself, it does not mean you have to be all boring and can't do anything with your look. You should be completely satisfied with the way God made you but you can also be free to create whatever look you want. Just make sure you are not following a trend, but rather expressing who you are.

You can change your hair, your weight, your dress code, etc, but just be sure to accept the things you cannot change, like your knock-knees. Make it a part of yourself, it is after all a part of your package that makes you, you. Also remember that just by smiling, you are already improving your look.

Your life

If you don't like your life make a list of what you can change and what you can't and all the excuses you give for not living your dream. You will find that that is all they are, excuses. If you don't believe it, go back to the pay offs chapter.

Everything you do must express who you are. If you are comfortable with your true self it will be expressed in every aspect of your life - your work, your financial status, your relationships, your dress code, your hairstyle, and any other way it could be expressed.

Have no fear, live every day as if it were your last.

Once you've decided who you want to be, you may find it a little difficult at first. There may be a few little belief systems that are restricting you like, "you're not supposed to", or "you have to", or "you must work a 9 to 5 job" or whatever. Make sure you know if these restrictions are valid or if they are just based on what other people think.

How will others perceive me being myself?

Because we have been programmed for so long about what is normal, what is accepted, what is wrong, etc, it is very difficult for people to see someone who breaks free of all those limitations. They don't have a clue what being themselves means because all their lives they have been told to stop being like they are and be normal. They are all trying so hard to fit into some crowd or another, just to be considered normal.

We have all been conditioned by the world in a different way and since everybody is trying so hard to fit into some crowd, nobody is being their real self so everybody ends up acting. To be our true selves we have to unlearn that conditioning. Look around you and watch how many people are acting. You will be amazed! You will find that what we think is real life, is just like a movie.

Friends who try to get us to be like they are and influence us in a negative way, are not our true friends. They are just people who have gotten lost in what the world thinks one should be like. It takes so much less effort to just be who you are and you will find that the type of people who are also their real selves, and allow you to be that, will automatically come your way. These are real friends. They will never put you down, criticize you or make you do something you don't want to. If there is ever a situation you don't agree on, you will end up finding that your real friend is only trying to help you and it is done with love, not with ulterior motives to benefit themselves.

When constantly looking for acceptance it is easy to fall into the trap of becoming anything anybody wants us to be, just to feel worthy. This could be very dangerous. There are many people out there with their own problems that are looking for somebody to manipulate and take advantage of. It is vital not to depend on outward influences to decide who you are, but to rely on yourself. If you have a sense of self and know who you are, nobody can tell you what to be.

It is in people's nature to automatically put everyone into a category and give them a label like cool, nerd, enemy, over friendly, loud, whatever. When you cannot be placed into a category, they call you crazy. As long as you are not completely wacky, they will like you because they are captivated by trying to label you and not being able to. That is when you are being yourself. They cannot understand it because you are not like anyone. You are not trying to be like anyone either. They admire it but don't understand it. They see that you are so confident, yet not arrogant. (The difference between confidence and arrogance is that confident people are being themselves and arrogant people are trying to be something they are not). Others see their possibility in the reality of you.

How will being myself influence others?

The most important thing is to be an example to others. Once again, try to be confident, not arrogant. When you are completely comfortable with being who you are, people will admire that and may release some of their own restricting boundaries. Other people may choose to stay the way they are because they feel safe in their boundaries. Accept them for who they are and decide whether or not you want to have their influence on you.
Real power does not lie in having power over others, but rather in giving people their own power back. You will notice that the satisfaction of getting others to see and realize their own worth, strength and wisdom is far greater than using them to value your own worth, strength and wisdom. This is the real meaning of dedicating your life to God, being a worker for God or being a lightworker.

When you are your real self, you have no more masks you are hiding behind. You may loose old friends but now you

will find real people like yourself who also have no masks and they will be your first true friends.
Even when you are acting in consciousness all the time, there will still be people who don't like you. Their own belief systems will make them perceive you differently. They may perceive you as a lawbreaker (you do what you want, despite society limitations), pretentious (you know everything), friend of bad people (you see the good in everyone), etc.

You may loose a few friends (which were not real friends anyway), but you will gain a whole lot more friends that will love and accept you, exactly as you are. When you have respect for yourself, you inspire other people to have that same respect for you.
When you love being yourself, you will love yourself, your life, and everything else around you, including other people. People will be so attracted to this love you emanate, it will fascinate them.
The most difficult part in trying to help someone is trying to get through their rigid belief systems. After all it is these belief systems that hold everything in place for them and that caused the problem in the first place.
When connecting with someone, think - "how does it feel to be him / her" and "what does your soul want me to tell you?"

How to be confident

Just realize who you are. You are so individual that no other person can even be compared to you. It is like comparing chalk with cheese. There is no better, there is only different. It doesn't matter if someone looks like you, has your smile, is better than you, thinner than you, etc. Only you can be you. There is no other person that can be who you are. You are unique.

You are made in the image and likeness of God. God is not like you, you are like god. He wants us to remember that

we are masters, not servants. You will discover in following chapters just what that means.
Our biggest gift to give is the gift of ourselves. **Although your presence is not needed, it is celebrated.** When you feel that nobody needs you, don't let that make you believe that nobody cares about you. **Your purpose is not to be needed, it is to share your presence**. When you are filled with joy, others will appreciate and enjoy being around you because you bring them up, out of their fear, pain and negativity.

By being yourself, you can help people realize who they can be and who they truly are. They say that good teachers don't try to put something into, but rather try to bring something out of, every student.

The Ego

The ego is often thought of as an oversized head or view of oneself. It is normally used when referring to someone who thinks they are more important or better than others. In actual fact it is the opposite which only appears that way. People who act in an egotistical way actually feel little, vulnerable and act in defense because they do not know how great they are.

Ego is not about thinking you are better than others, it is merely the protection program in your body - like a firewall. When we, as a soul, comes into the physical plane, we get a space suit (a body), which is programmed with the ego. It is this program which makes us forget who we are. It is the veil which holds all the stuff to keep you from consciousness. The ego blinds you from your real self. It is the program that creates the belief of separation. The ego is the mechanism that builds and protects belief systems.
The ego's job is to protect us, that is why it creates belief systems, fear, labels, masks, etc. It uses these little programs it has designed to predict the most possible outcome to prevent being hurt. It makes sure you always come first, no matter at what cost to others.

It determines what is dangerous and tries to warn us to prevent any danger. It is the source of fear, which is sometimes good but mostly distracting. It is good when it protects us from jumping off a building but distracting when it prevents us from living consciously.

It recognizes the body, material possessions, emotions, and everything the senses can perceive as real and is forever trying to protect these things and the belief that they are real. It is as essential to have an ego on this earth as it is to have a body. In fact it is part of the space suite package. It makes us believe that the illusion is real. If we didn't have it, the game would be over.

The ego gets undone little by little the more conscious we become. This is because the ego is made of beliefs and as they change, the ego disappears. It is not some evil power you need to overcome; you just need to overwrite the program.

The ego is so scared of you becoming conscious because then you will not need it anymore and it will be destroyed.
Identification with the ego gives it more energy; observation of the ego withdraws energy from it - as with anything. If you acknowledge that you are anything that is part of the ego, you are strengthening it. If you deny labels, beliefs, etc, the ego gets weakened.
So now that you know the truth, you can let the ego go. Acknowledge it but don't believe it.

Sometimes it feels like great effort to overcome the ego and remember what is real. The ego always has to be defended because it is not real and that takes effort. Love / consciousness is real and takes no effort to practice because it already IS, there is nothing to prove or defend. So stop trying to be conscious and simply quit trying to

defend the illusion / ego. By not defending the ego, consciousness is automatic.
Another way to recognize when the ego is in control is arrogance.
It is not arrogant to accept yourself to be as great as God made you. To accept your littleness is arrogant because it means that your evaluation of yourself is truer than God's evaluation of you.
The difference between being the best and doing your best is that with the first, you are doing it for yourself. This involves the ego. When doing your best, you do not care about winning and it is in the interest of everyone.

When you get negative thoughts or get pulled into the illusions, don't condemn it or get angry with yourself, just redirect it by remembering consciousness. The ego needs to be trained to see things from a higher perspective. You cannot get rid of the ego, nor do you want to, you just want to reprogram it to manual instead of automatic so that it allows you to use discretion from your real self.

Living in the now

One of the main reasons people find it difficult to be happy is because their minds are forever in the baggage of the past or in the worries of the future. This creates a huge amount, if not all of our stress. Stress is any situation, good or bad, that is difficult for you as an individual to process. It is normally something that you play in your mind over and over, to try and find peace with the situation. Most discontent is from unnecessary judgment, resistance to what is, and denial of the now.
By believing that everything happens for a reason and nothing is random, it is much easier to live in the now.

Past

Guilt, resentment, grievances, sadness, bitterness, anger and the inability to forgive, are all signs of living too much in the past and not enough in the present.
When you are full of problems from the past, there is no room for anything new to enter. There is not even enough room in the mind for a solution for the problem you are working on, to enter. We cannot keep hanging onto problems in the past. We have to accept them and carry on.
With some people everything about them is about what happened!!! They have so many memories clouding their vision. Stop living in your past and live in the now. We don't have to define ourselves by what we've been through. That does not have to make up who we are today. Find new things to define who you are today.

The past must be remembered, understood and then forgiven.

Future

If you are in the here and now, while your mind is in the future, you create an anxiety gap. Anxiety, tension, stress, worry, and fear are all indications that you are too much in

the future and not enough in the present. Most stress is caused by wanting to be somewhere other than where you are.
The mind creates an obsession with the future to try and predict how something will turn out. This prediction is normally very inaccurate and as with the past, the mind is so busy that there is no room for a solution to come in.

You have to just wait and see how things work out. Do what you need to do and make peace with whatever the outcome may be.
Don't allow the waiting to keep you in the future either. Just leave it until it actually happens. There are no problems, only situations to be dealt with now or left until they can be dealt with then.
Waiting is a state of wanting the future. Are you forever waiting to start living?
Make sure that you are not so busy getting to the future that the present is reduced to a means of getting there?

You can only ever have true peace when you have no desires. As long as there is something you want but don't have you will be restless. You have to live in the now, not in the future, then the future will happen anyway but without the stress.

If you live in the now, you will never depend on anything to make you happy. Being happy right now does not mean that you don't want things to change. The decision to change things does not have to come from being unhappy with the way things are, it is merely a preference to change it, choosing a new experience. If you want to change something, do everything you do with that intention, but don't expect that change to be the thing that will make you happy.
Surrender and accept what is happening in your life.
Ask yourself "what is lacking at this moment?" You will find that if you are in the exact moment to the second, you will find some peace. Think about how you feel when you are

absorbed in a movie, you have no interfering memories or stresses, you are totally in the moment. The same goes for the moment of a kiss, and watching a breath taking view.

If you feel overwhelmed by problems, take a second to think, "Do I have a problem right now? In this second, is there a crisis? What needs to be done right now? What is the worst that can happen and is it that bad?"
You miss out on so much if you are not in the present. It is something that we need to teach ourselves. The moment you realize that you are not present, you are present.

To be fully in the now, be fully present in every insignificant activity you do. Pay close attention to every sense and experience it like it is your first time.
Living in the now means to fully accept what IS and not blame the past or worry about the future. Stop worrying about why you are doing something and focus on how you are doing it.

Section 2

Know God

God

Contrary to popular belief, God is not an old man sitting on a throne in heaven with a lightning zapper in his hand and watching your every move so that it can be decided if you are worthy of heaven or damned to hell. He is also not some Supreme Being that grants favours if you beg and plead hard and often enough.

Having this picture of God creates a tremendous amount of fear. If God is like that then we have absolutely no control over what happens to us and unless we behave and do everything God says, we will be punished and sent to hell. We would live in constant fear of being wrong, being punished and of your life being made more difficult than it already is.
We get told that God is so great and powerful and that he loves us so much that he had his son die for us because we are such sinners. Makes a lot of sense, doesn't it. We also get told that we have free will but if we don't do it God's way, we will be punished. If God says we must do something a certain way and then says you have free will to choose how you want to do it, how can he punish you for doing it "wrong"?
How can God be so great if he is constantly punishing, jealous and angry?

All these views of God have been created by the leaders of the world, which are the governments and religions. Think about it. What is the easiest way to control people? Use fear, make people so scared of something and then convince them that you will look after them. This is the typical "problem, reaction, solution scenario". Using God was the easiest and also the most brilliant way of controlling people for their own agendas. They convinced everyone that they knew what God wanted. Only the priests can communicate with God and then tell you what he wants and what he will do if you don't do what he

wants. Makes God look like the boss and the church as the heroes. This way the people in the church are the experts about what God wants and can play with their own agendas, convincing us they are God's. If we trust the "experts" to do our thinking we are asking to be treated like mushrooms - kept in the dark and fed on $*#t.
I wonder what God has to say about all this. They also convinced people that they will look after them and that they are safe as long as they stick with the church and give them some money for all the hard work they are doing on behalf of the people. Sounds like a real good business plan. This way they can get money from everybody and at the same time, have the people of the world do exactly as they say. They even go so far as judging and punishing you on behalf of God.

On top of it all, the churches give us their specific books, which are all different to other religion's books, and are so jumbled that no one can understand them. This gives the leaders of the church free rein on interpreting the books as they wish. They also tell us not to read any other books not recommended by them, because they are so scared we will find the truth.
Religions and followings all over the world have created a certain image of God for the people so that people will do what they want them to do. Most religions are entirely based on fear. Everytime you ask a question you get told "we don't have the answers for everything", "don't question God", "you will know the answers one day when you go to heaven" or "the bible says you must just have faith". Shows you how much they don't know. They make you believe that you are not supposed to question God and you are definitely not supposed to question your beliefs about God. Do not challenge what you believe, God will punish you for even daring to say he might be wrong, and the religion you are following will reject and curse you. People believe that they must believe what they believe, even if what they believe is unbelievable. We are taught by the religions (to protect themselves) that whatever you

have been made to believe, do not challenge it and persecute anyone who does.

This God or perception of God is creating limitations, fear, dependency, guilt, anger, resentment, control and lack, which is not a very godlike picture.
Although all religions contain some elements of the truth and all believe there is a higher power, it has become so distorted by people's power agendas that it is difficult to find what is truth and what is not.

Now you may be thinking "so if everything we believe about God is false, then what? Is there a God, and if so, why does he allow this to happen and what does he really want?" With all these religions, how do we know who is right, every religion thinks They are.

So now that we know what God is not, let's explore what he IS.
The truth is that God is love, life, peace, joy, happiness, harmony and abundance beyond our comprehension. God is unconditionally loving, completely needless, nonjudgmental, non-condemning and non-punishing. God is not a singular person, but rather a great consciousness. God has no specific gender, size, shape, colour, etc, but can be anything and is everyone and everything. God is not a person but rather all that IS.

God is the "stuff", which is in everything and gives it life. God can also be described as love or light. God is everything. God is in you, in the dog next door, in the plant on your patio and even in the soil. Without God this whole place would not exist and it certainly would not be alive. God is the extraordinary thing called life.
We are made in the image and likeness of God because we are Life. We cannot be alive without being a part of Him. Life and God are the same thing. If you believe that you are alive, it is impossible to not believe in God. However, God

does not require anyone to believe in him because he IS, whether you believe it or not, is irrelevant.

When you live with the knowledge that God is everything, including you, you will find what life is really all about.

When you are in the mountains, see a puppy, watch a child play, look at a flower, etc, you are watching God because God is love, which is life. You can see how God is everything and how great God is.

When you find the God within yourself, that is your God realized self, also known as your higher self. It is when you see the perfection, beauty and wisdom that is you without all the masks and coverings. The single most important thing to know is that God is in you and manifested through you and the Christ consciousness is the knowledge of you being God and living in the path and flow of love, peace, joy, etc. Everything else is just minor details.

One

The reason the earth is like what its like is because people see themselves as separate from God and therefore everything else. This makes people selfish and they have no concern for how what they do affects others. If we realize that we are all one, we will take every living being into consideration in every little thing we do, because if it affects another, it affects us. When we realize that we are all one, you will consider everyone, and thereby serve everything, which is serving God.

We are a part of God and God is everything, that is all there is. The missing link in all religions is that God is all, he is not a person like us. Nothing else matters. When humans see themselves as **a part of God** as apposed to **apart from God** everything will change.

We are all a part of God the same way that every drop of water is a part of the ocean. The ocean is everything and everything that is inside it is still a part of the ocean. Nothing in it can not be a part of it. He is separate from nothing, is everywhere present, the all in all, the beginning and end, the sum total of everything that was, is now and ever will be. Our universe is merely a holder of all the particles God created in order to experience Himself - the totality of that which is.
Realize that because you are made in the image of God and everything is one (God), you are part of everything. There is one breath of life everywhere in everything; there is no plural - breaths of life.
Same as there is no plural waters, there is only one water and all water is essentially part of the ocean water. God is the spirit and you are an individual soul of that spirit.

Practice seeing everything as yourself. See the flowers as a part of you, see the homeless person down the road as a part of you, see yourself and everything as a part of God.

Envision "There I go again, being a blade of grass, being a policeman, being a mountain, being an angry person, being a mother, being whatever". Everything is in a state of being to experience being that specific thing and you are a part of it.

Illusion

There are a few really good movies that touch on the subject of everything being an illusion. "The Matrix" and "What dreams may come" show a good general idea of it (when you take out all the Hollywood movie stuff and look at the message). There are two illusions that we as earthlings have to recognize and see beyond. The first is the illusion of solid matter and the environment we are in.

Quantum physics has proven that matter is not solid. We always think of an atom as a solid particle but actually it is just electrons spinning around a point of gravity, a little ball. But even this nucleus is not solid and pops into and out of existence as much as the electrons do. Matter is completely insubstantial. The particles take up an insignificant amount of space in an object and the rest is vacuum. They have come to the conclusion that there is no physical thing on this earth (including the earth). A particle is not a solid thing, it is a wave of frequency. Everything comes down to light and energy. It is all just fast and slow light vibrating at different speeds. Slow vibrating light looks like solid things (bricks, sand, wood, etc) and fast vibrating light looks like air, sunshine and the light from your kitchen globe. Still it is all the same stuff. A TV demonstrates nicely how it is all just frequency. It can convert a "physical" scene into light (a picture) and then transmit it through the air as waves and then reassemble it again as a picture. That just shows you what an illusion this is.
Through various brain tests, it has been discovered that in the same way that we don't know when we are dreaming until we wake up, the brain cannot distinguish between a memory and a "real" incident. Its impulses are exactly the same. Therefore we think this illusion is real but when we awaken (become conscious), we will know that we have been dreaming.

If we could see matter as it truly is, we would see most solid objects as wispy fluffy stuff but our brain is convinced that “solid” looks the way we see it.

Above all that, the electrons in an object build up a charge and push the other electrons away before they have a chance to touch. Therefore nothing ever touches anything!!!. It has also been proven that because everything is a wave of frequency, it can be in any place or all places at the same time. It just depends what part of the wave you look at. Therefore you choose what position every particle is in.

Many quantum physics books will explain it in more detail if you are interested to know more. There is also a film / documentary called “What the Bleep do we know” and its sequel “Down the rabbit hole”, which is definitely worth watching.

The second illusion is all the pain and conflicting emotions we create for ourselves on a daily basis. Anything that distracts us from love and gratitude is an illusion. God is love and that is all there is. Anything that distracts us from that and makes us believe we are inferior, unworthy, limited, fearful, etc is pulling our awareness away from who we really are and gives us a false impression of ourselves. This can be anything we perceive as negative or evil. That is all in our illusional reality so that we have something that blinds us from reality - God and love. It is all part of the game to find ourselves again. This will be explained further in “why bad things happen”.

Religions have come up with the concept of a devil or Satan to explain why bad things happen. Satan is not a guy with a fork and horns, or an angel that was cast out of heaven and now lives to torment us and give us grief. The Devil or Satan is actually just a collective word for anything that keeps you from God or consciousness (knowing who you are). The devil is thee illusion (not just an illusion). The story about Lucifer being kicked out of heaven is actually a story about how you are not in heaven or God consciousness when you choose to be in the illusion. It is a metaphor in the same way that anything that does not express pure God (love) is sin. Sin is not about disobeying God, it is about denying God. Anything that pulls us into the illusion and away from God consciousness is sin. Therefore everything that is not love is sin. Being poverty conscious is sin (God is abundance), unhappiness is sin (God is happiness), loneliness is sin (God is fulfillment), unworthiness is sin (God is great), sickness is sin (God is health), etc.

It is not something that you are doing wrong and will be punished for but rather something you are not seeing and thereby are punishing yourself by believing your pain is real.

When you are distracted by things that are not real, you are not in consciousness and it feels like God (love) has deserted you. This is why they say the devil tempts us. The illusion tempts us with negativity. It is when we have forgotten to be grateful for the experience. Just see through the distractions again and you will be back in "heaven" or "God's kingdom", which is consciousness.

God cannot withhold good. God IS good. God can offer you an illusion to see if you will fall for it but essentially the good is always available if you let yourself see.

The illusion (Satan) is an opposing force of God, but is still a part of him. Nothing can not be God, God is everything. It is all part of his plan to see if we can still be in consciousness when we have all these things to distract us. If you replace the word Satan with the word illusion and Jesus with consciousness (that's what he symbolizes) when you read the bible, you will get a much deeper understanding. Notice that the word "evil" is the word "live" spelt backwards. Anything evil, is just something that is an illusion, and when somebody decides that something is evil, it is normally fear or active memory based. You can see how there is no such thing as evil; there are only things that we need to see through and remember who we really are.

Earth is just one small level of our soul's schooling. On this earth level, we learn that God is only love and that there are many distractions to show us what love is not, so that we can truly know what love is. Think about it. If you have always been with God, you only know love but you cannot know what that is until you experience its opposite. We are put here with no memory of where we come from and have to find our way back home (to God, to love). On earth we learn how to find love and how to stay in God consciousness, despite all the distraction around us. The world is a testing place that God has created to give us this opportunity to realize ourselves, which is him. God is testing us, and we are testing ourselves, to see if we will realize or remember our true nature (that we are part of God) or if we will get lost in material stuff (the illusion). It is our choice if we want to live in the material world or if we want to live in consciousness (knowing who we are). That is where free will comes in.

Only love and gratitude is real. Everything else is the illusion.

Christianity teaches that "you must let God be the center of your life". This means that you must always be conscious of your purpose (to find who you are) and of love (God) and not get stuck in the illusion. Acting in consciousness must constantly be on our minds.
Anger and fear put us straight into the illusion because the soul is made of love, and we cannot feel love when we are feeling fear or anger. This is how we get lost and fall off the path of love and consciousness.

When you have been through a certain experience you can have compassion with someone else who is going through it but you can see the illusion in it.

There is no use getting lost in the distractions from love, there is a deeper meaning behind it. Worrying is unimportant and there is nothing to fear. If you have experienced everything, you have become a master of this earth and can move onto greater universal lessons and explorations.

We have reversed reality and illusion. The illusion is that man is the victim and not the master.

We have been given so many ways to experience and perceive this illusion and make us think it is real. Emotions, the senses, material possessions, being born, dying, and being in a physical body are all ways that are being used to make us believe it is real. We had to believe it is real to get lost in it. If we were never lost in it, we could not seek who we really are.

The 5 senses

Anything that cannot be perceived by the 5 senses, like angels, ghosts, telepathy, intuition, etc is considered evil or occult by many people but it is not all that strange if we consider that only a small percentage of this dimension can be perceived by the senses. The brain receives 40 million images at any one moment but can only perceive 2000 of them. Imagine what all the stuff is that we cannot even perceive through the senses.

Consider for a moment what it would be like not to be able to see. Just because you can't see something, doesn't mean it is not there. What if you had some other senses like radar, or telepathy? Then your reality would be completely different.

Your different senses are just different frequency receptors. Each sense takes a certain frequency and converts it into something we can perceive. Everything is just a frequency and the really low ones are received by the skin, we experience them as touch. The higher

frequencies are received by the eyes and ears and we perceive them as sight and sound.
Therefore, the 5 senses are merely different frequency receptors and there are many frequencies that we do not have receptors for, so we can't perceive them.

Being born and dying

This is a concept that really tricks us into thinking that we are separate from God and that we are in a real place. If we were pure spirits coming from God and entering and leaving earth as we pleased, it would be a different story. The reason why we can't do that is because we need a space suite with all the senses to perceive this earth that God has created for us. We are taught to believe that when we are born, that is our beginning and when we die, that is our end. Actually it is merely a matter of entering this earth and leaving it again. Watch the film "K-PAX" for a good understanding of it.
Death is an illusion - the soul cannot die, it just leaves the earth.

Your body

As we have just learned, the body is only a space suite for the soul, so that it has the right tools or senses to experience earth properly. The physical body is an illusion to make us think we are separate from the rest of the breath of life or God. You get to stay until your space suite expires. This is when you die. You may get a renewal on your earth license sometimes if you die and come back or get healed from some terminal disease.

The ego is the program for preserving the space suit. It decides attack, defend, act in a certain way, etc as we have discussed earlier. You need to think with your soul, not with your mind because the mind will mislead you. Every emotion except love and gratitude, is a physical chemical produced by the body. Anger, fear and even excitement are chemicals. We can see how much adrenaline can affect us. Lust, pleasure and even happiness are all a result of endorphins, another chemical. Love, joy, peace and gratitude however are not chemicals but our only guide to what is real. If you stay with anything that expresses love and gratitude, you know you are on the path of consciousness.

Focusing too much on your look, job, car, or any material stuff is focusing on the wrong body. That is the illusion. You should focus on your real self - the spirit of love and consciousness. The physical body is merely a reflection of who you really are. What's on the inside shows on the outside.

As we discussed earlier, we can change water with certain words. Being 70% percent water, the same applies for us. Our attitudes, emotions and projected energies determine everything. If you are positive and live in love and gratitude, you will become a beautiful crystal. When you are beautiful within, you become beautiful without.

By increasing our knowledge of our real selves, we are able to control our physical bodies, like the masters do. That is where controlling your emotions, ignoring pain and even walking on water or levitating comes in. Miracles are just being able to go beyond the illusion and using it to assist your soul. You are stronger than the body.

The body is just a space suite so that you could come here to learn these lessons. The earth is like a simulator, it was created to give us lessons, but it had to be convincingly real for it to work. One of the blessings or powers is to know that you are in an illusion so that you can relax.

We are spirit, not physical flesh. To live only in the consciousness of this visible body of flesh is spiritually retarding. What we are doing here is temporary and not who we really are yet we treat life like it is the only experience we have and ever will have.

Our goal is to realize that we are not the body and are stronger than anything it can threaten us with in the physical world. "The lord is your shepherd," means that if you stay conscious, no harm can come to you.

Why bad things happen

God created evil on earth so that we can see good. If everything was just good, we would have nothing to compare it to and nothing to distract us from it. That is the test, to find God amongst all the negativity or illusion. If everything were good all the time, you would want to stay in the dream and not wake up. The whole point is to wake up; we need misery to do that. Misery is actually a good thing, because it makes us search for answers and thereby find God. It is in desperate times of our lives that we go searching for answers. Think about it; when everything is going fine, nobody cares less about God or the answers to the universe. When your life is really messed up, you are confused and that is what makes you search for answers.

God has given us free will to come back to him and stop suffering. God doesn't want us to get lost in the illusion by taking it so seriously, he wants us to follow him and get out. He wants us to become aware of how everything works and that there is no real pain or suffering.
We are in a movie. After we die, none of it matters anymore. The only thing that matters is whether or not we have learnt the lessons we were meant to learn. Enjoy the love stories as much as the horrors and actions. That is all it is, a movie. The world is just a stage and you are playing a role. Remember this in times of joy, in times of sorrow and in times of anger. Play your part with conviction but remember with a smile inside you that you are just playing a role. Start seeing everyone being exactly as they are meant to be and believe they are. Shopkeepers are playing the role of shopkeepers, policemen are playing the role of policemen, etc.

Just observe for a minute how animated this place is. Just look at how we come onto this earth. Two people have sex, a baby (a new space suite) grows inside the woman and becomes a porthole for another soul to enter. Wow! We take for granted just how unbelievable that is.

Become a watcher. Watch and observe everything around you, even yourself, like watching a movie. See how everything is an illusion and that it has been made as a learning ground.
When we start observing and watching our experiences, we can stop being involved in them and in the pain we are feeling. We realize that there is always a lesson involved, which only makes us wiser and stronger.

We have been given the experience of dreaming so that we have some way of understanding this concept. When we are dreaming, we are in an illusion but we think it is real. Only when we wake up, we realize that it was not real. Nothing that happened in it damaged you (your soul) in any way.
Know that when something goes wrong, your life is not over, it is just altered. It is just an opportunity to become stronger and less involved in the illusion.
You might think that it is impossible to live like this. The point is not to ignore the world but rather to not let it get to you. Still live your life but don't get involved in the emotions of it. All you need is consciousness.

Getting stuck in the illusion is the only thing God does not want you to do, as that causes pain. God wants you to be in consciousness and know what it is like to be Godly, allowing all your actions to be through love. No sin (falling into the illusion) can be committed with the intention of love behind it. Therefore, sins are errors committed under the influence of ignorance.
"Sinners" are just like everyone else. They too are looking for happiness; they are just confused as to how to get it. Don't curse the sinner, even if you do not agree with what he does. He has his own lessons to learn.

Bad things like cancer, bacteria and illness also have to exist. They are a means of getting off this planet when it is your time. At some point your space suite has to expire so that you can go home. If everything were nice and happy here, nobody would want to leave. Of course it is sad to loose a loved one but once again, play your part with conviction, remembering that your loved one is rejoicing because they have gone home.

Sometimes people only contract to come in for a short period. For example a baby will have an agreement in the spirit world to only come in for a short period to maybe learn one lesson but also to fulfill a lesson the people involved needed to experience. Deaths never happen unless it was that person's time to go back. Be happy for them. In a near death experience it was not your time, you may have just had to learn to appreciate life and learn that there is more to life than you think.

The illusion of need is the principle illusion that all other illusions are based on. We believe that we need other people, money, protection, material possessions, food, etc. Those are just needs of the body, not of the soul. The soul needs nothing. It is after all a part of God, which is everything. There is nothing lacking.

Consciousness

Becoming conscious is the process of finding out and knowing who we truly are. The more we live and express love, joy, abundance and gratitude, the more conscious we become and the more we grow spiritually the better we start to understand the true nature of God, man and the creative laws of the universe. Becoming conscious is about gaining awareness. When you are able to see that you are everyone and then experience life through other's eyes, you will know why they are like they are, where their problems are coming from, what they cannot see and you are able to tell them what they need to hear. When you are in ultimate consciousness, any situation is viewed as an extraordinary adventure that is part of being on this amazing place called earth.

As we have learned, everything is light. People have layers of veils over their eyes so they cannot see all the light, only limited amounts of it. These veils are our beliefs, masks, labels, etc. The more we work on removing all this baggage, the more light we can see. Everytime you have a realization, you have removed another layer.

Some people focus their consciousness only on one aspect of their lives but fail to do so in other areas because of their beliefs and issues. They might be very good in relationships but cannot keep a cent due to poverty beliefs or vice versa because of beliefs from their parent's relationships. Some are sick all the time but wealthy and others are smart but cannot control their tempers.
The more light we can see, the more we know what is going on around us and the more conscious we become. Only when you see the pure God in everyone, all the time, and see every being as absolutely perfect, are you in pure consciousness. Yet it is not about just being in consciousness, it also about knowing and remembering that you are consciousness.

Awakening to consciousness is like living in a black and white world, then God gives us colour and we think "WOW, now I am awake", then God gives us smells and we think " wow, now I am awake, how could I think I was awake before?" Then come tastes, then concepts, feelings, understandings, experiences, etc. There is always so much more to learn. You always think you know everything until you learn something new.

God is consciousness

We have already learned that God is all. He is the great consciousness. He is the Infinite being that has expressed himself as an infinite number of distinct beings or units of consciousness. This includes us as well as any thing with a consciousness, even a cell. This includes anything that knows that it IS. Man is, in his true nature, an individualization of God. I am God being me, and God loves Godself as me. God is not a bigger version of us but we are a smaller version of God. God is all-powerful but we are not. We can only become powerful when we join God. Joining God has nothing to do with either being baptized or saying a little prayer at church to be "born again". The only way is to live it. One of the first steps to "joining God", "becoming conscious", "inviting God into your life" or "being born again" is to invite the feeling of love into your body and allowing yourself to listen to the guidance.

You will always be you, as an individual, whether you are conscious or unconscious, in body or in spirit, etc but the ultimate goal is to find your way back to God or "the Father's" house and to be the true self-expression of the infinite. God is expressing himself through us. We are like the prodigal sons who have forgotten who we really are and have been lost in the illusion of material possessions and now we need to find our way back to the father, which is the consciousness of knowing who we really are.

Life is the process of awakening. It is the process of becoming. It is part of the process of knowing that one has become what one always was. It is the process of rejoining the inseparable (God). And that is not a process of actual rejoining, but of simply knowing that separation never occurred. This is what being born again really means. It is not about asking God to be a part of your life, but rather realizing that he already is and then living according to that. Being born again is about knowing again. It is re-membering, re joining the one. The knowing again is the awakening. You have to become one with God to experience knowing. When we join God, that is when we will be conscious. Conscious of ourselves, of others and of how this whole place works.

Consciousness raising is converting from being away from God into being one with God. Realizing who you are and that you are a part of God, is consciousness. All we have to improve is our knowing. When you are "in the presence of God" it means you are in consciousness - open to receiving and giving of love.
Jesus said, "I and the father are one". This meant that he was in God consciousness, he could see the truth in all. The Christ in you means the true consciousness in you. Love or God turns into You while You turn into it. You just need to focus on living in love and watch your life change. Just as God just Is, in the same way, I, just am. That is the "I AM" consciousness.

God does not need your approval, he is everything. It is up to you to live in happiness or consciousness or in misery and suffering.

Becoming conscious is realizing your purpose on this earth, the purpose of the earth and the whole life thing. It is about the joy of knowing that you are not just a mortal being that lives and dies and that's it. By becoming conscious you start being in this world and not of it. You watch it from an outsider's perspective and observe how unreal it is. Consciousness comes when you can see the full picture and therefore are able to live life as smoothly as possible because you are open to receiving the messages. You can adjust and work around everything, you never run into life head on. You know that when you are pulled into the illusion and away from love, gratitude, joy, etc, your ability to see reality ceases and thereby all your powers cease.

The feeling of being in nature is the feeling of being in consciousness. That is why a weekend away is so relaxing and refreshing. It's the energy we use to restore our batteries.

Unconsciousness

Unconsciousness is seeing the impermanent as permanent, the painful as pleasurable, the non self as the real self and what's not real as real.

People in the illusion are very unconscious and what is known as "worldly" people. They focus on material possessions and struggle to obtain love and happiness. They are filled with doubt, frustration, fear, jealousy, hatred, anger, lust and competition and they don't realize how pointless it all is, where the conscious person is at peace because he knows that everything is as it should be.

The biggest unconsciousness, which causes suffering, confusion, and all kinds of 'bad' things, is from people not understanding each other. They never consider others as a conscious person would do. It is all based on the self and on physical satisfaction.
At a lower level of consciousness you cannot predict how your actions will influence your future and therefore you make silly mistakes that cost you in the future. Also, the lower the consciousness level, the less you understand the concept of seeing the God in other people. You do not have to be very conscious to see that there is at least some good in every person and that they are also a living being just like you, with feelings and problems of their own. When you cannot even see that there is a living being

inside a body it is easy to hurt other people. This is the level that murderers, rapists, etc function on. They have no concept of the fact that all people have a family, feelings, and a life and their unconscious acts heavily influence them. They just see people as bodies. They cannot put themselves in another person's position. Physical violence only happens because of deep unconsciousness.
Our degree of unconsciousness is increased when we are in pain or suffering because we get pulled into the illusion. When you are pulled into fear or anger, you cannot perceive how someone else is feeling, increasing your likeliness of acting in an unconscious manner.

There is also collective consciousness, which is dictated by the people around you. That is why certain people become friends or gravitate towards certain areas; they have a common consciousness and therefore feel like they understand each other. This can actually end up pulling you into a lower consciousness because when some people are negative or fearful, they pull others into that with them. Being negative grows collective unconsciousness. It is easy to get pulled into collective unconsciousness like sickness, limitations, lack, poverty, etc but stay in the truth and don't let them pull you down. Don't judge them for it; just don't get involved in it. You can still show compassion, understanding, etc, but see it from an outside perspective.

When you start becoming conscious you may find it challenging to relate with unconscious people because they don't understand. You start finding that conversing over pointless mundane conversation is boring and you have nothing to say to them. When you speak, people who are not on your level will not understand you. They will call you crazy and tell you to stop being so deep.
The only thing to do is to be the example - be joyful, stable, peaceful, etc but most of all, be yourself. Still live in the world even though you live beyond it. People will only listen to you and follow your example if they can

understand and relate to you. If you don't act normal, they may even call you crazy and try to save you. They just don't understand.
God created different levels of consciousness so that not everybody would see the truth. If everybody knew, the game would be over because we all would have found God. We have to let people find it on their own, don't give the game away unless they ask you and are genuinely interested. Some people enjoy being in ignorance, it makes them feel safe and protected. Remember that we are also here to experience and not everyone's experience involves becoming conscious. There are certain things you can only enjoy when you are ignorant, ignorance is bliss. When you are conscious it is more difficult to enjoy having meaningless conversation, getting drunk all the time, using drugs, going to clubs, having meaningless sex, etc. So let them enjoy their experience until they are tired of it.

Levels of consciousness

There are so many different levels of consciousness and perceptions. We perceive our reality according to our consciousness. Your reality depends on what frequencies you have the ability to perceive according to your beliefs. This is shown well by using the example of a pun. The perception of a phrase with two meanings will depend on the observer's beliefs, active memories, etc and they will understand it in a certain way. Another person might see it completely differently. For example if someone says "Love your neighbour", a person with a lower consciousness will think "I don't love my neighbour, he's an idiot". A person with a higher consciousness will know that it means you must see the God in everybody and only express love, because that is all that is real.

Consciousness is determined by your ability to perceive love. Very unconscious people have relationships based purely on sex and generally don't have much love in their lives.

Everybody is in a different reality and a different consciousness and therefore a different frequency. They all create their own realities according to what they believe and some things are just not in some people's realities. Some people believe that they can have anything they want, so therefore they get everything they want. Others will never even look at a fancy car because they believe that they will never have it. Something will only ever be in your reality if you believe it is. You cannot perceive anything you don't believe in. It might still be there but you will not notice it. You may drive past a billboard screaming the answer to your problem every day but if you do not believe there is a solution, you will not see it.

The higher frequency something vibrates at, the more conscious it is. Therefore rocks are very slow vibrating (i.e. dense) and therefore very unconscious. They are being held very firmly in the 3rd dimension and can only experience this dimension. At the same time they are what makes up this 3rd dimension. The higher something's frequency, the more effect it has on its surroundings and are able to change its surroundings. E.g. we can consciously change the appearance of a rock (low vibration) by polishing it. The more conscious we become, the more we are living in the fourth dimension because we are out of the illusion or 3rd dimension. When you are living in consciousness, you move into a higher dimension and once again your mindset creates your reality. Evil, fear, etc cannot touch you because you are out of the illusion where these things exist. You can only experience love, respect, worthiness and kindness.
We will discuss more about dimensions later.

It is easy for someone of higher consciousness to recognize when an act is done in lower consciousness but a person in lower consciousness has no ability to recognize that there is anything beyond them and their beliefs. They cannot recognize when they could learn something, or that someone knows more than they do and

can help them. They completely identify with the ego. If someone doesn't have an absolute desire to become conscious, they never will be. Even though you tell someone that they can have everything, they will tell you that they just don't have time for that right now.
Explaining being conscious to somebody who is not conscious enough to understand that there is such a thing is like explaining music to a deaf person who does not know there is a hearing sense. They just cannot perceive it.

Consciousness comes from experience and you have to have been in a certain situation to understand it or else you have nothing to relate or compare it to. The more experiences you have, the more conscious you become. You will see how someone who is naïve is someone who has not had a lot of experience and someone who is wise has had plenty of experiences, especially difficult ones.

Just as with anything in life, there are certain stages you need to go through before you can get to other stages. For example you need to crawl before you can walk before you can run. If you skip certain stages you will not have full or comprehensive understanding of anything. One needs time to think about small ideas and concepts so that one can start asking questions and appreciate the answers when they are given. When the student is ready, the teacher will come.

There are various stages of becoming conscious: (These are just the stages I have come across and I'm sure there are many more. They also do not necessarily have to be strictly in this order.)

The first stage: Being completely unaware of other people having feelings, lives, etc and doing whatever you want without considering for a second or caring about how it may influence anyone else. They are unable to perceive love.

The second stage: The majority of people - they are just going about their every day lives with no awareness of who they are or what they can achieve. They do however realize that most people are essentiality good and do consider other's feelings.

The third stage: You start becoming aware of what you are eating, the chemicals you are putting into your body, etc. This is where you start using natural remedies, assessing your diet and looking after your body.

The fourth stage: You start wondering if there is more out there than we know about and start exploring new ideas. This is the stage where people start wondering about "new age" stuff. They have started questioning the rigidity of religion and the validity of fairies, angels, dream catchers, candles, tarot cards, etc. All those esoteric, "new age" stuff.
Before people reach this stage they are normally very religious (any one counts) and absolutely believe that all esoteric stuff is either hog wash or just plain evil. Then an event may happen in their lives to make them start questioning if there is maybe more out there that they do not know about.

The fifth stage: Here is where you find that angels, psychics, tarot cards, channeling, crystals, etc do have some validity and you start telling everyone of your new discovery. This is the "I believe" stage. You may even start playing with some mind power tricks like magic and discover black magic and white magic. Most people get stuck here for a long time before moving on.

The sixth stage: You start learning about things like everything being an illusion, all being one, coincidences, reincarnation, etc. This is a very confusing stage because it feels like you are learning so much so fast and you struggle to keep up with yourself. You are learning at a fast pace but don't have enough understanding to get a

picture yet. You just cannot figure out the manifestation thing though. You read books like its going out of fashion and are intrigued by talking to other spiritual people.
The seventh stage: You start getting a nice understanding of all these concepts but also start noticing that you are going beyond what other people know and they don't want to hear about it. Your family starts thinking you are crazy, you start loosing friends, you feel lonely and very depressed.

The eighth stage: Things start coming right in your life and you are more in a positive mindset than a negative one. You don't see the miracles in your life as something supernatural anymore but rather as the natural projection of living consciously. Here is normally where you become dedicated to finding the truth and becoming enlightened. Your need to tell everyone ceases and you just live a peaceful, harmonious life. A lot of inner searching and being alone is preferred as apposed to the outer searching of stage six.

The ninth stage: You start realizing that you create your own reality and can live any way you want. You dedicate your life to living the best way you know how to. Money is abundant, relationships are good and you see God in everyone. You are at peace with yourself.

The tenth stage: Your personal desires are fulfilled so now other people are starting to notice you being an example of how they want to be. People are automatically attracted to you and you find yourself giving them guidance and counseling. You will find teaching becomes exhilarating but you know that you have to wait for people to ask first. You start preparing ways to get your message out there.

The eleventh stage: When you go public with your message. You start a group, become a spiritual councilor, write a book, etc. You are making a contribution to lifting earth consciousness.

We are immortal spirits entering into the illusion or earth program. Like in the film "The matrix" they are programmed to wake up from the illusion by a telephone ringing, we have set certain triggers to wake us up during this life. There will be certain events in your life, that have been put there just to wake you up and let you see real reality a bit more.

What are the benefits of becoming more conscious?

To become conscious, there must be a yearning for something better beyond material stuff. We can make our lives so much more meaningful by seeking.

The point of becoming conscious is a rebellion against lack, limitation, disease, control, loneliness, failure and unfulfillment. You will no longer settle for other people's beliefs and fears holding you back. Conscious people often get called rebellious from childhood because they refuse to accept all the injustice in the world and other people's beliefs and limitations.

Finding our powers is far greater than any material treasures.

Spirituality and consciousness

Being conscious and being spiritual are two completely separate things. People often relate being enlightened with being spiritual. Being spiritual only means you believe there is more out there than what you can see, it does not mean you are at one with God or act in any way pertaining to that. You are not spiritual if you do not behave spiritually. Behaving spiritually means behaving in love. Therefore consciousness goes far beyond spirituality even though it is a part of it.

How to become more conscious

The first step to becoming conscious is to realize that there is such a thing, that there is more to what you see and that there is a higher purpose. We have a built in desire to find the truth and once we remember that there is truth, we will automatically seek it. Our whole purpose on this earth is after all to remember God and our real selves.

When you start seeking truth, you will find that it is like opening a can of worms. It is like in "The Matrix" when Neo has to choose between the red pill and the blue pill. Nothing will ever be the same again. It is a difficult but very rewarding path to follow. You will start wondering about things like; what are belief systems and what is real? What is destiny and what is free will? Does anything mean what we think it means? Who am I? What is my purpose? Why was I born? Where do I go after this?
You will find the answers and they may be completely different to what you expected and create a whole new string of questions.

There are many different routes that may lead you into consciousness. Some find it through religion, some through meditation and others through working on themselves and practicing self-study. They all could eventually lead to emotional freedom and thereby consciousness. It is imperative to release old emotional baggage before you can become conscious. The emotional stuff keeps you in the illusion and prevents you from seeing through it. Emotional baggage makes you feel fear, anger and all the other emotions that do not lead to love. Your happiness and love will always be on condition of your emotional state. When you are conscious, no emotion can prevent you from feeling love.
Realize and apply the fact that everything happens for a reason and then accept everything as it is. This already will eliminate a lot of emotional baggage. You can allow a challenge in life to awaken you, or you can allow it to pull you into an even deeper sleep. The worst or most detrimental emotional baggage is the feeling of unworthiness because this makes you feel unworthy of getting God's messages or being one with God.

Create a spiritual journey where you observe every moment, be in the now and see the wonder. Write it in a journal. Practice the art of being grateful in every situation.

Always follow what takes you into love. As soon as you are following something that leads you into fear, you know you are on the wrong track. This is how you find consciousness. You will recognize something that takes you backward by when you are feeling fear. Just follow the love or anything that gives you love. Love is the threadline that runs through everything. It is the rope that has been given to lead us to consciousness. Love will show you the way. It is a very fine line to stay on.
Love is light and illusion is darkness. Darkness is merely absence of light. Love is the flow that you need to tap into. You can only see what you are doing (be conscious) when you are in the light.

In remote controls, genuine crystals are used to transmit and receive messages between the remote and the object it is controlling. In the same way, if we become crystals (like water does when exposed to love and gratitude), we become receptors of the truth. The truth can communicate with us. If we are filled with negativity, we cannot receive the truth or messages but if we are in love and gratitude, we are open to receiving them.

Consciousness involves seeing yourself as one with everything and therefore treating everything with love. When you can do this and can see the good in everybody, you will know what makes them tick. That is how some people can get through to people and others can't, because they know how people think. If you are only "psychology conscious", it is easy to use it in a negative way. But if you are "psychology conscious" and "love conscious", you will never do anything to harm anyone; you will use it to help them.

Consciousness comes in realizations and one of the best ways to open and still your mind to get them is through meditation. Meditation helps you to release emotions. It also teaches you to be still so that you can be guided. It is the stillness, which one needs in order to hear the messages which are distorted by the mind and emotions. When you are still, you can perceive the truth. Books and experiences are other tools that we have been given to help us become conscious.

Let God speak to you

God speaks to and to everyone, all the time; it's just that not everyone listens. He is not a beaming voice from the sky but rather the vibration of love that you can tune into and then you can see everything. You will see subtle signs to help you along your way, you will see coincidences happening in your favor, and sign boards seem as if they are made just for you. There are many subtle ways God speaks to us.

There is a story about a guy in a flood sitting on his roof and praying to God for help. A boat comes past and shouts for him to get in but he refuses and says that he is waiting for God to rescue him. Then a helicopter comes over and tries to save him but once again he refuses saying that he is waiting for God. In the end he dies and asks God why he didn't help him. God replies that he sent help via boat and helicopter but the man refused. This is a good example of how God speaks to people and them not listening.

You need to start looking for your signs from the universe to tell you when you are on track. You can even ask your angels to use certain signs for you. It can be a symbol, number, name, picture or anything that has meaning to you. You will start seeing these signs everywhere, especially when you think something is not working out. That is your sign that you are on the right track even when you think you are not. These signs will be seen in the most random places like billboards, cars, t-shirts, etc. People, especially little children will say things randomly that you can take as a message. Look out for them and recognize them. A listening attitude can work wonders in your life. Watch the coincidences unfold in your favor. You will be amazed! If you have difficulty believing it is possible, try it for three days. Pretend that you believe that God is everything and gives us signs and after 3 days you will know it is true.

People can tell you all about their own experiences but you will never really believe it until you see it for yourself. It is like the joy of riding a water slide. You have to experience it to know it.

Coincidences

There are no coincidences in life. Everything happens for a reason and exactly as it should, every second of every day. Even going to the grocery store at a certain time is not a coincidence. You might have needed to go there to bump into someone you have been thinking of for days, or you might get a pamphlet on your car window for something you have been looking for.

You might have noticed that whenever something big happens in your life, "good" or "bad", that it becomes a major turning point in your life. Everything happens for a reason and that reason is to make you who you need to be and to experience and learn certain lessons you need to learn or experience. What you think is bad might not always be so terrible if you look at it in retrospect. For example look at Nelson Mandela. Was it such a bad thing for him to go to prison? Sure the experience of it was not in the least enjoyable but look where it got him. If it wasn't for that key event in his life, he would not have become president of South Africa and he certainly would not have been able to accomplish all the amazing things he has done. The same goes for any terrible event that happens to anyone. The death of a loved one, being assaulted, loosing something, or experiencing pain in any way. You never know what the bigger plan is.

Your life is always working for you whether you know it or not. Sometimes it brings you what you want, and sometimes it works to keep you from what you think you want, until you can see that that was not what was best for you.
Sometimes bad things need to happen to push your life a certain way and make you who you are. Every now and then something bad happens to steer us away from something and into something new. It might just be a block to say, "OK, enough of that situation, time to take what you've learned and move on".

You can only ever have true peace when you realize and decide that everything in your past happened exactly as it should have to make you who you are today. By knowing this you will not hold all that resentment and anger anymore and will become a better, freer person. Through forgiving others, we forgive ourselves.
When someone has done you in, in any way, you can either make yourself a victim or you can move on and recognize that you will understand it later.

Obstacles

Everything on earth works in opposites. We have the one so that we can recognize the other. We have light and dark, good and evil, love and hate, rich and poor, ignorance and consciousness, easy and difficult, love and fear, etc but we also get a whole spectrum of varieties in between. Because of duality we have been given a whole lot of things that are opposite to God consciousness but are also a part of God. It was all put here to distract us so that we have consciousness to search for. If everything was consciousness we would not be able to search for it and that is the purpose of this whole earth set up.
Because of this, you may find that with many things you try to accomplish, there is resistance. The road to getting what you want is often harder than you anticipated it to be. The harder you try to love, the more rude people you encounter. The harder you try to make money, the more

expenses come. The harder you try to get your business going, the more obstacles you run into.
When a seed starts growing, it has to push through ground but then finally sees the light. We are the same as a seed reaching for the light. When you start being a seeker of the truth you have to overcome a whole sequence of obstacles to realize properly that you are in an illusion, only love is real, etc. Therefore you will constantly be tested to see if your consciousness is stronger or if your emotions are still ruling you. It is just a matter of practicing.
You need to practice to stay in consciousness more and more until you can stay in it permanently. It's a process not a sudden event. So every time you pass the test of not getting involved in the situation, you will be given a stronger test to see if you can maintain it. Very soon you will find life becoming easier and easier not only because you are guided, but also because you can see so much clearer when you are not blinded by emotions. You must be determined because the soul can survive anything. The more you try do to something good, the more you are eliminating karma, guilt, worry, etc so life automatically becomes easier because you don't have to deal with all that anymore.

You will find that as you become increasingly conscious, lessons will bounce back at you faster. If you criticize or judge anyone, you will find that only a few moments later, you will be judged for doing the same thing. This is just another way of practicing love and seeing love in everyone and when your judgments bounce back at you it is just a reminder. Admit, forgive yourself and then try to be more conscious the next time.

Do not keep denying that you are conscious. Even if you think you have a long way to go, consider yourself growing consciously. Consider it a journey instead of a destination to strive for. By affirming that you are conscious, you will grow consciously and create it. Wisdom is not having all the right answers; it's having all the right questions.

Enlightenment

There are many spiritual groups selling enlightenment and giving it all kinds of definitions. They all give a prerequisite to becoming enlightened and inevitably their master is so called "enlightened".
The truth is that enlightenment is not a destination but rather a process. Every time you have a realization, you are enlightened and the more you can stay in the light of love, the more you will experience enlightenment. It is the path of eliminating all darkness from one's life. One cannot become enlightened, we can only experience it. It is even possible to be in enlightenment today and slip out of it tomorrow. In fact that is most often the case. It is very difficult to stay in it all of the time but through constant perseverance the goal is attainable.

Experiencing enlightenment has nothing to do with what you do with your body or your mind. It has to do with what you do with your soul. When you find peace, joy, gratitude and love in every moment you are experiencing enlightenment. The more you live in enlightenment, the more you will realize that there is nothing to do, but everything to be. Whatever you do do, will be done in joy and love. When you are in enlightenment your soul purpose is to make others see the divine in themselves and bring them to peace. You want to make everyone realize that they are perfect. You will often hear new age people use the phrase "Namaste". This means "the God in me sees and honours the God in you". You will see that all these "Masters" who run around desperately trying to convince people and convert them into enlightenment have actually missed the point. They get so busy that they forget to be in love, which makes them slide out of consciousness and enlightenment. Spiritual progress is not measured by knowledge but rather by the love you give.

In the experience of enlightenment you know, without a doubt that you are a part of God and that everything is made of love. You will know that even though we as humans experience sorrow, pain or any other hindering emotions, they are all an illusion.

The secret of life is that dying is merely leaving the earth after your visit and knowing that you were never really separated from God, that you are a part of him and always will be.

Does it mean you are always healthy if you are enlightened?

Does being healthy mean that you have nothing wrong with your body or is it when you are happy and in a place of joy and peace no matter how things are?
When you are in a place of love, no pain or illness can survive because they are of much lower frequencies and are there because of your emotional issues that have been stored in the physical body. When you are in consciousness you also are very aware of the body only being a space suite so anything that happens to the body is of little importance or concern to you. Even if there is pain or illness you can separate yourself from it in such a way that you do not even feel it. Also you may realize that whatever illness you have, it is your body's way of expiring so that the soul can leave. Some dedicated masters can even leave their bodies at will.

A part of being conscious also includes being health conscious. When you eat healthy, do exercise and look after your body, you are developing a health consciousness. Even though the body is a space suite, we need it to fulfill our earth tasks. The cleaner and healthier the body is, the less distraction one has. Physical pain or discomfort can be a huge distraction from consciousness as it makes us focus on the illusion. Exercise and a healthy diet allows the mind to be clear and light as apposed to being dull and heavy when filled with toxins.

Since the body is part of the illusion, our attitudes and beliefs have a lot to do with our physical health. We can either make ourselves healthy, or we can make ourselves sick depending on our beliefs. Although this means that we have the power to heal ourselves, it does not mean we don't need medical intervention. In most cases a positive attitude is all that is needed for a better recovery.

Section 3

Know the universe

Religion

Everybody has for all eternity wondered what is beyond our sky and why we are here. That's the people of the earth's biggest question. Every now and then somebody comes along and says, "I know" and forms another religion or following.

It all started with people knowing that there is something beyond what we can perceive in this world. Religious and all spiritual people believe there is a higher power but that's where many get stuck. Instead of aiming to become like it, they worship it and look for orders from it.

It is sad that a lot of people who follow a church are often people who have been taught that they are sinners and can never forgive themselves for anything. They often have a need for God to punish them so that they can feel better about themselves. Guilt is also a way of alleviating yourself of the responsibility to be in control of your life and moving on from your past. It is comforting to believe that the church is looking after you and that if you follow their rules, you can live happily ever after in your mansion in heaven. This relieves us of our responsibility of finding our own salvation through constant effort.

Religions are held together by followers, not leaders. They are people who are too afraid to listen to themselves and would rather have someone else in charge. They use religion as a crutch and rely on God for everything while blaming the devil for everything that goes "wrong".

The picture of this is why many people choose to stay away from religion and spirituality. All they see is the neediness, weakness, naivety and the hypocrisy coming from religious people. They preach about love and God but are very quick to judge anyone who is not "as good" as they are. They fail to see the God in everyone because they believe him to be a human like figure apart from us. It is a pity that people's only reference to spirituality is religion. So when something spiritual happens in their life, like a near death experience or seeing and angel, they realize

there is something more that they didn't believe in and turn to religion where they can easily get mislead.
Religious people get told that anything they do wrong is caused by Satan but that they will be punished for it personally.
All religious teachings are fear based. If you don't do what "God" says, you will be punished. This gives the leaders of the church free rein to punish people on behalf of God and for people to judge each other. Any form of punishment reinforces the idea that blame is justified. There is no such thing as sin and nobody is a sinner. Calling yourself or anyone else a sinner, discredits the God within you. The only punishment there is, is the punishment you create for yourself by not acknowledging that you are a part of God. By denying your magnificence, you deny yourself happiness.
Religions who revolve around the crucifixion teach that the power of the Son of God is born of pain and suffering. They believe that you have to be in pain and make sacrifices in order for God to love you. God does not want obedience because obedience implies submission and submission implies that there is something better than you are and that you are flawed. We need to focus on the resurrection because the lesson is that you are already immortal and nothing that happens to you on earth is real. The truth cannot die.
Even the Ten Commandments are not laws, they are advice. It is not about obeying God, it is about following his advice to make your life easier.
There is no point in worshipping God by telling him how great he is because he has no ego to accept or perceive this praise. To praise God is to be one with him. You can only make God happy by being happy because you are one with him.

Religious teachings are all based on one book which has been rewritten so many times that it is all distorted apart from the fact that they are taught to read it literally. They are told that "clever wanna be's" over analyze the bible instead of just taking it like it is. They are told not to question God or the Bible, just believe it. They will do anything in their power not to tick God off. This belief again presents fear and therefore closes us off to love.

The truth is that we have to analyze it because it was written in a coded way in order to protect it through the times when the witches were burnt and any information with them. Think about it. There are so many stories in the Bible that just don't add up if you take them literally. Who did Cain marry if Adam, Eve and he were the only people? Why would God need Adam's rib to make a woman if he made Adam from nothing? Why would God create an angel that could overthrow him, isn't he supposed to be all-powerful? It is all metaphorical. The info in the Bible is still quite accurate but has to be read on a different level of consciousness. Replace the word 'Satan' with the word 'illusion' and replace the word 'Jesus' with the word 'consciousness', and you get a whole different picture as that is what they represent.

Here are a few examples of what the Bible is really talking about:
There is a story about the angel Lucifer being kicked out of heaven and sent to come and rule earth. At the same time he is God's opponent and they are at constant war between good and evil.

The real meaning here is that God created evil (which is the illusion) and put it on earth so that we can experience remembering Him through all of it. God is everything and there is no thing that he competes with. We only see it as something that competes with God because we have a choice to choose either consciousness (good) or illusion (evil). What is light without dark? How can we recognize a saint if we don't have a villain?

Adam and Eve were created and put in the Garden of Eden. They were told not to eat from the tree of knowledge of good and evil because they would die. The snake is said to be the most cunning animal that the Lord had made. It told them that if they eat from the tree of knowledge they will not die, for God knows that from the day you eat from it your eyes will be opened, and you will be like God, knowing good and evil. So Eve thought about how wonderful it would be to be wise and ate from it. She then influenced Adam to also eat. Their eyes were opened and they knew that they were naked so they made themselves coverings. Eve was blamed for it all and told that from now on she will be subject to Adam.

It actually means the following:
The fruits mean consciousness, which allows a person to be able to judge between good (consciousness) and evil (illusion). If they ate from the fruit they would not die in physical form but rather their unconsciousness would die and they would become conscious as God IS. The snake was the symbol for the illusion, it was not an actual snake talking to Eve, and it was symbolizing how people in the illusion might try to influence you. So God was not giving them a law but rather revealing the options of consciousness or unconsciousness to them. "Adam" means "mankind" in Hebrew and "Eve" means "human beings". So they were not only two people on earth and this story did not happen to anyone specifically, it is a metaphor. Them realizing they were naked means that they realized that what they had done before, was in ignorance and they felt guilt and shame. Someone then added on their own interpretation of the story and made women the cause of all strife so now they have to be under the command of men. This belief has caused chaos in human society and only now, thousands of years later are women starting to recover from it.

The problem with the Bible is that when they found the scrolls they didn't understand it so it was just put in any random order. It is so mumbled and scrambled that it is difficult to understand. Apart from that it has been rewritten so many times that it does not say the same as the original text does, kind of like playing the game "broken telephone". There are also all different editions, which contradict each other and different versions leave out different parts.

Until recently, anyone who was not a Christian (according to the definition spelt out by authorities) was tortured or beheaded. In these days, when every spiritual person was called a witch and burnt at the stake, there was a huge amount of fear generated amongst the people while the leaders or governments only became more powerful. They scared the people into choosing unconsciousness and not much real information survived the ordeal. The information that did survive had to be encoded enough for it to survive so now that we are finding the hidden scrolls everywhere, it is difficult to unravel them.

Many people, who call themselves Christians, condemn the new age movement as the work of the devil or servants of Satan. They were led to believe this by their powerful leaders. True Christians should be known for their love, not by their condemnation of others. The secret is to do what Jesus would have done in every situation. It is important to listen for all calls from God, not just the ones he gives you in the Bible.

According to most religions God keeps changing his mind all the time. In the sixties dancing was considered evil - "how dare people throw themselves around like that, it must be the work of the devil." Then in the seventies it became a beautiful expression of oneself. Some people say it is against God's will to fix birth defects while in utero but after the child is born, medical intervention is fine. So now, how did God suddenly pass the work of the devil as the work of God? These are all perfect examples of how we are controlled by what the "leaders" of society think and say. Religions are spreading their word as the word of God.

Religious people often get taught that only the leader of the church can communicate with God. This automatically puts him above every one else. Why would God only talk to some people? God talks to anyone who listens. It will not be a booming voice from heaven but rather by looking for the joy, love, gratitude, etc in every aspect of every day.

Spiritual consciousness has nothing to do with one's religion, but rather with one's awareness and understanding of one's true self. It is important to realize that all religions are on a particular level of consciousness but should not be condemned because they are a very necessary stepping-stone. The point is to pass through them and use what you have found to be true, not to get stuck in them. Never just take what anyone says as gospel, and especially not anyone that claims to have the knowledge exclusively, like from a cult or a channeling. It is universal knowledge and is available to anyone that is open to receiving. You have the power and privilege to know the truth directly from God.

Religious people also get taught that if you behave and do what God says (according to them) that you will go to heaven and if you don't, you will definitely go to hell where you will burn in the fire for all eternity. What a terrifying thought. If I believed that, I would rather do "what God says" and stay out of trouble. This belief leads to feelings of guilt as we find it difficult to satisfy God all the time while life constantly throws obstacles and challenges at us. They also get told not to ask questions and never doubt what God says. What a great way of controlling people!!!
Thank God (literally), that is not how it works. Heaven and hell are not places but rather a state of being. When you are living in unconsciousness and experiencing all kinds of negative stuff (the illusion), that is hell because it is difficult and you think that God has neglected you. When you live in consciousness and "walk with God", that is heaven.

What happens when we die?

When we die, we all go to different spirit worlds depending on our consciousness. There are many layers of worlds all on different frequencies. They all exist in the same physical space that we know i.e. within our universe (and beyond) but we cannot see them because they vibrate at faster frequencies. These are what we call dimensions. We are in the 3rd dimension which is physicality as we know it. Everything is 3D. As you go into higher dimensions things are created by thought, not physical matter and you can change it at will.

When we die we do not automatically and instantly become conscious and have all the answers, we just go to a resting-place and are still in the consciousness that we were in while on earth. We have to find it on earth, you don't just get it when you die, that is the test and purpose of earth. So many people don't even want to explore spirituality because they think "why bother, I will know everything when I die?" They are only wasting time and fooling themselves. Now is the time! We are on earth purely to grow our consciousness so how can we just be given it when we die with no effort on our part?

Please note that this is not a judgment on religion but rather an effort to let you see that the truth is not to be found from groups or elsewhere, it is inside you.

Reincarnation

This is a very controversial issue because religious people have such active memories around the word. They have been told that there is no such thing and you are not even allowed to investigate the possibility of it. Reincarnation was even deleted from the bible because the controlling bodies believed that it would hamper the growth of the church because people would think that they had forever to be saved, and would postpone the process. Why would you bother doing anything the church tells you God wants if you can just come back and do it right next time. There is no motivation to do the right thing. So the church created the concept of hell. This way they could threaten people with the thought of eternal condemnation and scare them into seeking salvation. They were told that they better go to church every Sunday and do what "God" says; else they will be condemned to an eternity in hell where the flame never goes away. Sounds horrible! Nobody wants to go there.

With a bit of investigation it is obvious that we live many lives. It has been proven by children having memories, psychologists finding hypnotized patients telling them about it, etc. There are so many case studies.
How is it possible to experience all we need to experience and become a master of earth in one life? That would be like going to school for one day and graduating. We live lives of killing, being killed, being poor, being rich, being a slave, being a king, and many more. There are so many lives to live and experiences to experience; it cannot possibly be done in one go.
To the unconscious person the realization of that would mean they can do whatever they please and that if they are good in the next life, they will be saved; but to someone who understands karma, you will know that is not the point.

Karma

Contrary to popular belief karma is not a punishment and reward system. It is the latest trendy word on everybody's lips who is vaguely involved in the new age movement yet there is so much confusion about it.
The word "karma" means "action". From there we can derive that it has something to do with what we do. All we do on earth is to have experiences.
Everybody who comes to earth needs to complete the cycle or circle of karma to experience all there is to experience. It is not a punishment and reward system but rather just a way of keeping track of what you have learned and of making sure you experience all there is to experience. Remember that we need to experience all experiences there is on this earth to become a master of it and be able to help other people get out of the illusion and into consciousness.

The karmic balancing of pain and pleasure has nothing to do with punishment or reward. It is not even about actions and consequences but merely provides us all with a balance of experience through which we can evolve and grow as spiritual beings.

We only build karma if our intention is bad or ignorant. If you for example kill someone accidentally, it doesn't count as you doing something bad, just as an experience of killing someone accidentally. That is when God uses you to just be the one to help that person off the planet. It might just be a lesson in overcoming guilt for you. Recognize that it is not necessary to feel guilty because you did not intend it and it is all part of what was meant to happen. People who have no conscience on the other hand are severely stuck in karma. Lessons will keep being thrown at them until they learn to feel the pain that they inflict on others. Karma is simply the process of being given a

lesson over and over if necessary until you have learnt it and are ready to move on.
For example: You will keep choosing abusive relationships (a karmic cycle) until you learn that you are worth more than that and gain the self respect to pull yourself out of it. You cannot become conscious if you do not realize what a magnificent being you are, made in the image of God.
When your lessons do come along, stay strong and don't let it get to you. Remember also that you might have contracted that role for someone else's benefit.

People that are not meant to know or have not completed their major karma cycle will not be led to consciousness, because they are not ready. They have not had all the experiences yet or have not learnt to move on from a lesson. As they start reaching the end of their cycle, they will start being introduced to the truth. Therefore just by reading this book, it means you are being introduced to consciousness so that you too can end your cycle of painfully living according to karmic laws and come into your full potential.
That is also why we cannot live by other people's lessons and experiences. We have to experience for ourselves in order to learn and get through that lesson. The only way to know and to understand people is through experience. Reading many books can speed up your process because it introduces you to many points of views so that you can see the all round picture rather than just your own view or some group's view. You can also learn from books what the purpose is and make the experience easier so that when you have the experience, you can recognize it and learn from it the first time so that that lesson does not have to be repeated.
It is important that we must learn from the first experience and not get stuck in it so that we have to repeat it.

The more conscious one becomes, the smaller your lessons will become. These are just little reminders of the lessons you have already learned to keep you out of the

illusion. People at a high level of consciousness are too conscious to create new karma for themselves by doing something stupid because they have already learned that it is not real, nor is it beneficial to soul growth. They know that only love is real and fully live according to that with gratitude. As realized spirit they know that we must convert all negative energy into positive energy and would not create negative energy intentionally.
That is why they will not be given difficult lessons. They don't need big reminders. The smallest example will pull them back into consciousness. So for example, if they have slipped into the illusion of arrogance they will only need someone telling them and experience a little humiliation rather than having to loose everything before they learn. The more conscious you become, the easier the lessons become because you are more conscious and catch on faster through awareness. You also have the intuition to avoid it.

When you have completed the cycle of karma and have experienced all there is to experience, the result is to become conscious. A few people have however been born into this world in this life with no karma. They are doing a second round. So if karma were a circle, these people would be overlapping the circle. They have come here to help everybody awaken and complete their earth lessons. They have no karma because they have already learned everything and completed the circle and are only here to help others. Jesus was one of these people.

Only actions of love, mercy, justice, kindness and peace are the ones that will get you out of karma and into freedom. All other desires or rewards are false. They come from greed, power and money. These only create more karma and keep you in the cycle for longer. It is like driving on the road where it is easier or driving in the bush where you keep getting whacked by branches and falling into potholes. The sooner you learn to stay on the road of love, the sooner you will stop being given difficulties.

We are being tested constantly but not on our power to control, abilities to be the best or any physical achievements, but rather on our ability to love one another unconditionally.

Duality

Duality is the law of opposites. For every thing that exists, there is an opposite to balance it. Joy and sorrow, light and dark, up and down, hot and cold, good and bad are some examples. This is so that we can experience. If there was none of the one, we could not experience the other. If there was only light we could not compare it to darkness so we would not even recognize light as anything. Duality is however only an earth thing. There is no such thing as duality outside of earth or in the spirit world. E.g. joy and sorrow (there is no sorrow outside of earth). It was especially designed as part of the earth experience so that we may know who we are, compared to who we are not. As we discussed earlier, bad was only created so that we may see what good is and thereby see what God is. Keep in mind that this "bad" that was created is still also a part of God though.

Outside of earth there is only one, the one, who is God. He is everything, there is nothing else.

When you are in consciousness, you are one with God and are balanced. Therefore you step out of the duality and karma. The law of duality cannot exist and automatically disappears.

Contracts

Before coming to earth you agree to a contract with certain souls to help them as well as yourself experience certain lessons. It specifies exactly what type of lessons you will experience, what the experience will be and who will be "to blame".

It is often the souls that love you the most, that agree to help you with your hardest lessons. They are often the ones that you will have a great disliking for in this life because they make your life so difficult.

Some souls are contracted to come only for a short period in order to reawaken somebody like in the event of the death of a young child. The parents seek answers and thereby may be led to finding the truth and becoming conscious. Remember that bad things happening in our lives can be the trigger to making us seek and finding consciousness.
Whatever happens in your life, accept it as if you have chosen it because in the bigger picture, you have.

Jesus

Jesus was a good example of someone who came here with no karma but purely to help people become conscious. He was merely one of the prophets to show us how it should be done but instead of listening to him people started worshipping him.
Jesus was completely self realized and knew that this was all a hologram. That's why he could walk on water and do amazing miracles. He said, "I am one with the father". But they all thought he was just being arrogant. He was the Son of God and walked with God, the same as anyone can. It just means you are conscious and have become one with all and therefore one with God.
The story about Jesus dying on the cross could be literal but there is also a symbolic meaning behind it. The dying on the cross is the death of the physical and being reborn into consciousness. He rose from the death of the old and was resurrected into the consciousness. It was a symbolic way of showing us that you have to become uninvolved in the space suite before you can see beyond it. He said "God forgive them for they know not what they do". This was a way of showing us how people behave when they are unconscious. It does not mean they are wrong, it just means they are ignorant to love.

Christians often refer to Jesus as "Christ". Christ is merely the Greek word for "blessed" or "anointed". Therefore the word "Christ" just means "conscious".

Christians are told that Jesus died on the cross for their sins because they are such sinners. This places a huge amount of guilt on people. "Dying for our sins" only means he wanted us to see beyond the illusion. He wanted to show us how consciousness changes your perceptions and takes your focus off the body. As discussed earlier, the word "sin" means acting in unconsciousness. Therefore "dying for our sins" is merely a way of saying that he showed us how we can overcome unconsciousness.
Jesus was not the saint of all saints, or the only person ever of his status. Actually every culture or religion was given their own example. The Indians were given Paramahansa Yogananda, the Tibetans were given the Dalai Lama, the Hindus were given Krishna, the East was given Buddha, etc. God gave each culture and every corner of the world a good example, somebody they can relate to, so that they too could have the opportunity to become enlightened.

The story of Jesus is the prime example of what we should strive for.

Mirroring

At every new age conference or talk there is usually someone taking about mirroring. The theory is that every situation you are in is a reflection of yourself. So if you keep coming across rude people, you may have to evaluate your own attitude toward people.
The idea is to ask "what can I learn about myself from this experience?" Often things that we notice in other people are things that we have not come to terms with in ourselves. You might choose a partner who expresses a lot of anger because you are unable to express your own.
I do believe this happens a lot because people get upset when they see something which they reject in themselves, although sometimes it is a matter of reflecting your beliefs and not your actual character. Everything in your life is because of what you attract and the people in your life only play out for you what you believe. They are just

teaching you about yourself. People treat you the way you treat yourself.
So when you believe that nobody loves you and that you are all alone, you project that and it creates a personal law that has to sustain that belief.

I don't believe however that things always happen for the sake of mirroring. Everything is not necessarily a reflection of you. Sometimes it is just showing you a lesson you need to learn or a situation you need to learn how to deal with.

Cults / False prophets

The bible says that in the end of days there will be many false prophets to lead us astray. There are so many people in search of answers now that all kinds of followings are taking advantage of it. Therefore many new "religions" are starting that are based on the new age teachings in order to "catch" the "seekers". They all think that they have the full picture but their focus is normally on money and lacks the teachings of love and gratitude.
It is very important not to get stuck in these groups but rather to take what you can from them and use it to build your bigger picture, then move on. They often do have some truth but also go off the path quite a bit.

How to recognize them

- There are a few very obvious trends that they all follow:
- These groups can be recognized by the lack of love in their teachings and their obvious domination of the ego.
- They are also fear based and do not encourage you to read other books. You will find that they teach you about fear but subtly hold you by fear like telling you that if you do not do certain things you cannot be a part of the group anymore.
- Their courses are often done in levels so the more advanced you become the more your ego gets the satisfaction of being more important.
- There is often a leader who is said to be enlightened and everybody in the group follows him / her blindly.
- They use money to keep you dependent or involved with them. They teach you some selling techniques, and call it manifestation techniques to get money and then say that they have taught you how to manifest and be abundant. The more money you make, the more expensive courses they offer you.

Also when you become an instructor you can make easy money by offering the course to others. Eventually you become wealthy and will not even question their authority.

- They promise or rather sell "enlightenment".
- Sometimes they sell you a "healing" modality first and then once they gain your trust, feed your mind with their own agenda.
- Even though the group is all about enlightenment and abundance there is normally more squabbling and politics within it than in the government. They are also normally very poverty conscious with only the main guys having money.

More and more people are seeking spirituality and are in search of enlightenment, so they are easy targets for power hungry cults. All they have to do is promise you enlightenment and then make you believe that that is what they are teaching you.

Some of these groups will tell you that the more confused you are, the closer you are coming to self realization. Some even teach their followers that other people will be against their group because their egos are preventing them from seeing the truth. This prevents them from even being exposed to the truth because they think everybody is below them. It's ironic that it is their egos that are convincing them that they are self-realized. They don't want to be wrong. It is easier to follow that and say "I've made it, I'm self realized" and stop there than to keep working on yourself.

Self realization is not about that, it is about knowing yourself without all the emotional garbage and the ego. Seekers who don't work on themselves are easily manipulated and attracted by cults or false prophets.
The line between consciousness and limiting consciousness through getting stuck in groups is so fine. It can only be determined by feeling, not by mind. You

need to trust your instincts to know what is right because they will convince your mind that feelings are wrong. Go with love and self worth, never believe you are nothing and do not matter, as some of them teach.

Any organization that sells self-realization (i.e. asks unreasonable amounts of money for enlightenment), even if their intentions are good, stifle people's ability to find the truth.
The only way to find self-realization is through experience and meditation and concentrating on love.

It is important to follow the group that you think you can learn from but when you have learned what you needed to, move on. Never get attached to any group.

Meditation

Meditation is the only way to practice stilling the mind. It allows you to unpack baggage so that emotions do not come in your way any more. It allows you to experience God without the distraction of being on earth and of the senses. It is a way of experiencing the feeling of death before you die and realizing that there should be no fear of it.

Why do we need to still the mind?

You often hear people say "The answers are within you, stop looking for them everywhere else". That is the absolute truth. Your soul remembers who you are even though your mind does not. Meditation shows you that there is more to what you see and is the porthole to experiencing what is beyond the senses. It takes you to an in-between state of consciousness where we can get "blinks" of reality. These blinks only open for a limited time and come in small steps so that we can fully realize and comprehend the truth step by step. Meditation is observing an inner place, looking for answers.

We need to still the mind because it is the only way we can listen to guidance, asses situations properly and become more aware. You can see everything as a watcher would from his perspective. You learn how to not be involved in a situation and to see yourself as just playing a role. This makes life become easier in all aspects. Relationships improve because you can see the other's perspective. Situations become easier to handle because you can see all aspects involved and don't let your emotions blind you. Decisions become easier because you can see the whole picture without emotions and then asses which decision would bring you closer to who you are. Tasks become easier and quicker because there are no obstacles and running into dead ends.

When we meditate, the speed we vibrate at raises to a higher frequency as we are eliminating our material concerns, which keep us in the third dimension. When we are in a higher frequency, receiving messages become easier. When we meditate, we teach the mind to be still so that we can hear and recognize the truth in any situation because there is no clutter, no active memories and no fears distracting us.

The mind needs space, that's why we worry. By worrying we play situations over and over in our minds in order to find clarity. The mind is always trying to make space and clear out clutter. Meditation is the way to clear it. It is the same feeling as watching the mountains, the ocean or a fire. The mind becomes clear and free.

This is true communion with God. Communion with God is meditation, not eating bread and drinking wine in church.

Through meditation we find that God is always there, never away. We can just tune into him whenever we want. Meditation helps us to stop thinking so much and helps us see our real selves through all the clutter.

How?

Firstly find a quiet spot where your senses especially hearing and sight will not be distracted. Sit quietly with your eyes closed and just watch what goes through your mind. Don't follow any thoughts just watch them. If there are many thoughts, that is called outward meditation, which is a way for your mind to unpack and sort out baggage. It is very good stress release and is an essential part of meditation. When your mind has completed packing out you may go into a state called transcendence. You will find yourself completely aware but with no past or future thoughts. Just stillness, like watching the ocean. This is the part where realizations come and the mind practices to be calm.

If you struggle to go into transcendence, you could have a lot of baggage to pack out or constant stress in your life creating new baggage. Don't try to make anything happen,

just let it happen. By trying you may be stopping it. There are a few ways to improve your ability to transcend. One way is to repeat a mantra and think about going deeper and deeper (like to the bottom of the ocean, except it can always go deeper). The other way is to try looking through your eyelids, like looking at a 3D picture.
You will realize that you are in an empty space. It is like being in space. It does not feel like you are sleeping, you are completely awake and aware. Here is when you find peace from plaguing thoughts even though you are having thoughts about the big room or space you are in. The difference is that these thoughts are very in the now, not past or future. This is the place where you listen to God and the stillness. You will become the watcher. Everything is in the now and you are watching it unfold.

This exercise should be done for about 20 minutes twice a day to get the mind good at being still and watching.

In a different type of mediation called contemplative mediation, you can choose what emotional baggage you would like to release. You can find out what your active memories are by simply focusing on something specific during meditation and waiting for memories to come into your head. When they do, don't dwell on them, simply acknowledge them and move onto the next one. Some examples of things you can focus on include love, relationships, trees, anger, water, spiders, etc. Think about your fear of spiders. Just sit still and watch. A memory will suddenly pop into your head and you will know where that fear came from and then you can release it.
Think about your role and patterns in the relationships you have had. A flood of memories will come into your head and you will start seeing a pattern of how you behaved and why. It probably came from something in your childhood.
This way we can realize and correct our active memories and belief systems that make us keep going around in circles and not get anywhere.

Love is a powerful one and might send you on a bit of a journey. The feeling of being overwhelmed by love and all your memories of it is amazing. It can even make you feel like you are floating!
You can also do an exercise where you visualize light or love pouring in through the top of your head and flowing into your body. It dissolves all negative beliefs, body illnesses, etc and lifts you to a higher frequency.

When you still your mind, it is like resting the mind. If you focus between your eyes, you are resting the mind there. Focus here and stare through it. Stare into the blankness until something appears. Don't put something there, simply wait for whatever is there to be revealed to your consciousness. The most common image people see is a blue flame and a feeling of ultimate love comes with it. After a bit of practice your mind will learn to be there all the time, even when you are busy.
To stop being a slave to your mind, you have to find the off button. When you are the watcher, it is no longer controlling you. This is difficult in the beginning and takes some practice.

You can make every moment a meditation. Just live in the now and observe everything happening to and around you. Follow a dog, watch the sunset, look at a child play, climb a tree, see God in everything.
The ultimate meditation is when you are in it constantly. Wherever you go, you make every moment a meditation. You see the ants running on the pavement, the flowers blossoming, the faces of people you walk past all as a part of yourself. See yourself as being them.

Intuition

Intuition is that little voice inside you that tells you if you are doing the right thing. The right thing may not always be what society believes it to be but rather what is in the best interest of your soul. It is our destiny calling.

It is a feeling rather than a thought and is completely unignorable. It is a feeling so strong that it becomes a knowing. You just know something and cannot explain it.
Everybody has it, yet we cause ourselves a lot of karma (repeating of lessons) because we do not always trust it. Trusting it is something we have to practice because it takes faith. Sometimes it seems as though our intuition has led us along the wrong path but most often you will realize that in the long run it was definitely the right path.

Fortune telling

Tarot cards / psychics

Everyday life promotes a lot of fear and anxiety, causing us to spend most of our thinking in the future trying to predict the most possible outcome so that we can be prepared for it. This, preventing us from being in the present, easily allows us to be tempted by psychics and fortune telling to help us predict this outcome we are so desperately searching for. Knowing the future helps relieve our fears and gives us some hope to a brighter future.

Psychics can tell you things about yourself or about past events or even pass on messages from loved ones but they cannot see your future because only lessons are destined, not every event. You can change many events. It is a good thing that we cannot see the next day or into the future, if we could we would probably chicken out and go jump off the first bridge.

Tarot cards, astrology, psychics, etc can help you see the bigger picture but they cannot do the healing for you. We often wish to just get out of the pain and move onto the next thing but it takes time to heal and many experiences need to happen to make us realize why we had to go through such pain. It takes time to see what the purpose was and how it has helped us in the long run. Don't run away from the pain, it is only when we accept it that we can move on. There is no skipping it. Psychics can just give you false hopes if you trust them with your future.

It is normally thanks to the need of getting rid of pain that we seek for answers. It is unfortunate that so many people that start seeking, land up in the hands of psychics, channelers, etc because they don't realize the damage they can do by giving people false expectations or dreaded outcomes. Even though their intentions are good, many of them are at a very early level of becoming conscious and don't even nearly have the full picture. The better ones will

not tell you about your future but will rather give you guided messages.
It is vital to look for answers yourself and not to depend on others to provide it for you.

Magic and curses

Both magic and curses are only intentions put out from someone. Whether they affect you or not is your choice. It can even be a subtle thought of someone wanting harm to come your way. It can only affect you if you let it. Simply put a conscious shield around yourself and deny it the privilege of coming near you. It is only an illusion after all.

Free will / Destiny

This is one of humanities biggest confusions. There is one side of the debate that states that everything is destiny even to the extent of how often you blink. The other side states that if this were true we would all just be robots and there would be no point to life. This side believes it is all free will and everything is completely random.
The Bible says that we, as mankind are unique in the fact that we have free will. Yet some psychics, astrologers and prophets claim to be able to see the future which means that there must be certain things that are going to happen because they are in our destiny. A very good movie that explains this is "Time Machine". The scientist keeps going back in time to prevent his beloved from dying but no matter what he does she still ends up dying.

After much research, I believe our destiny consists of certain lessons, which include certain events but not necessarily every single little event. Events can change according to whether you have already learned that lesson or if you need another opportunity to learn it. When in unconsciousness, we just plod along and need to be shown the same lesson several times before we can move onto the next lesson in our destiny. When you are conscious enough to realize that you are being shown a lesson, you can learn it quickly and move on. When you begin to see your destiny or life purpose, it becomes much easier to create that and go straight there without all the blockages trying to push you in that direction. That is why manifestation is linked to consciousness. You need to be conscious enough to see your lessons before you can create your own reality and eliminate obstacles.

Certain lessons in our destiny give us frustration to motivate us into a certain direction. You may feel a desire to do something or a need for change. That is your destiny pushing you. It does not just happen, you need to follow that urge and go with it. That is how you create your own destiny and thereby your own reality. If something is not in your destiny you will have no interest in it and if you pursue something and it does not work out, it was only meant to get you somewhere else. It was just a stepping stone. That is why you cannot just sit back and wait for something to happen. You need to get off your butt and do it. Also do not get stuck in the "what ifs" or "should haves". Everything happened exactly as it should have. Your free will is your attitude. You can decide if you want to accept it and have a happy life, or if you want to fight, resist and be in anger, guilt or frustration all your life. That is how you choose between good and evil. You can choose the conscious path or the unconscious path. You can choose to awaken or to stay in the illusion where it is safe but limited.

If everything were planned for your life and you could just sit back, you would have no power and would not be responsible for your life. You are responsible to learn your lessons, have a good attitude and become conscious. You have to make that happen. Very few people are determined enough or have enough willpower to control their destiny but the rewards are great if you can.

Why do we get choices and how do they fit in?

Choices are merely opportunities to stay in your rut and repeat a lesson or to move on and learn from the previous lesson. That is why change is so important. How many lessons can you possibly experience by living the same boring life for 50 years because you are too scared to loose your security? Live and learn. There is so much to do! We are here to experience. We cannot experience things like the feeling of touch, the taste of chocolate, the freedom of flying, etc anywhere but here on earth so enjoy it.

When we are on the path to consciousness, we even get guided messages to tell us which road to take to move onto a better experience and get out of old lessons. We start learning lessons so fast that we become increasingly conscious at a very fast speed. Experiences and lessons bring consciousness and awareness.

Time

From early on in our lives we are taught that everything runs by time. We are taught how to use a watch and read time and before we know it, our lives become one big schedule of events. Yesterday is the past, today is the present and tomorrow is the future. We live by the past and work for the future. How did people live before the clock was invented, before time as we know it existed? Why is time so important? Does it really matter or has it defeated the purpose of living?
Living is all about the experience, all about the **now** and we have forgotten how to live in the **now**. We have forgotten how to live. Wouldn't you live very differently if you could never know the time or if you had to be told that you only have a limited time left?

According to quantum physic studies there is no time and everything exists all at the same time. Everything that has happened, is happening and is going to happen, has already happened and is already set out.
They say that this is because not only is everything set out and has already happened, every possibility of everything that could happen, has happened and any path we could possibly choose is available for us to take.
They say we do not live many lives at different times but rather parts of the same soul goes out into all different parts of time as bodies and we live them all at the same time! Going with the same concept, just in this life, you are being born, learning to drive, reading this book and dying all at the same time.

It is like every time you take a photo of something you suspend that moment in time. You can go back to that moment any time you want in memory and therefore that moment always exits. So now if you take a photo of every second of every picture on earth, all time will be suspended.

It could be explained somewhat by using the channels of a television as an example. If the television is the all / God / whatever you want to call it, just because there is more than one channel it does not mean there is more than one TV. All moments are on different channels on the same TV. It's just a matter of which one you choose to tune into and be involved in.

That's quite a lot for our physical brains to get around.

We know that in the universe there is no concept of time as our time is merely measured by the earth revolving around the sun and is a completely man made concept. We also know that when we ask for something from the universe, we have to be time specific because out of our dimension, there is no concept of time and 5 minutes and 1 year is all the same.
Spirit sees time as a physical coordinate specifying the location of an event. It is just a number that goes with a file containing that event, a bookmark. Spiritual time is measured in moments.

However it works is quite irrelevant to us stuck here in the third dimension. Rather we should focus on not being free of clock time but to be free of psychological time. Being free of psychological time means to be free of the time wasted worrying and thinking about irrelevant things and try to live in the moment as much as possible.

Section 4

Using it all

Manifestation

So now that you know how it all fits together, you know the rules of life so you no longer have to swim upstream. When you live within the laws of the universe, life becomes much easier because you can stop bumping your head and running into dead ends and actually start achieving what you want.

Manifestation is all about using the laws of the universe to make your life easier. When we become conscious we can stop wasting time by repeating lessons and get to our goals much faster. We know how to recognize the signs leading us into our destinies. Manifestation, however, is quite complicated and there are many factors involved. Let's start with the basic understanding.

In the movie "The Secret", they explain that we can have whatever we want if we just know how to apply the secret of life, which is the law of attraction. Whatever we attract, through our thoughts, we will attract into our lives. The things we think about most will manifest into our lives.

Thought is energy and every thought has a frequency. That frequency is sent out in physical form and attracts a like frequency. The more you think a thought, the stronger that reality becomes.

Most people, however spend a lot of time thinking about what they don't want instead of what they do want. The law of attraction cannot differentiate between you wanting something, or not wanting something. It merely responds to the feeling you are putting out. So if you are feeling negative all the time, that negativity will become your reality. You are given what you focus on most, so if you think life is terrible, that is the way it will be.

An affirmative thought, however, is hundreds of times more powerful than a negative thought.

People might say, "I didn't attract the car accident or my house burning down" but you did. It sounds scary but

actually it is quite liberating. Emotions are the amazing gift we have to let us know what we are attracting. You need to feel what you want.
The rules are, you must ask for what you want and the universe will answer. The key to make it happen is to receive it. To receive it one must act as if you already have it, you have to come into alignment with it in your reality.
Sometimes what you want will just appear and other times you will be given an idea as to how to make it happen.
Start by focusing on what you are grateful for to shift your energy to the good things in your life.

Manifestation and consciousness

It is however a bit more complicated than "The Secret" makes it out to be. Consciousness plays a massive part in manifestation; the law of attraction is just not good enough on its own.
God is the energy that runs though everything and that everything is made up of. It is all that Is and is everywhere. It is completely abundant and completely limitless.
God is ALL-POWERFUL. He is everything. No thing can be without being God. God is the medium (a universal power) that flows through our minds and translates into form and experience. Even the most unconscious among us who have no awareness of God, are still a part of God. It is impossible not to be, but you can only use the power of God if you believe in the existence of that power.

Now, if God were the ocean, you would be a drop in it. You, as the drop do not have the same power as the ocean does but when you realize that you are a part of the ocean, you can tap into the collective power of it. Unlike the drop, however, you are not limited to your circumstances but have the power to change them. You have the ability (and the gift) to be able to use this collective energy.

You just need to let God's love flow and stay in consciousness. When you are in consciousness your thoughts are positive and the energy around you is the same and only greatness, joy, abundance, etc can be expressed.

God is your supply

We mould our future and our reality every second of every day. Therefore, when you are in consciousness, God is the source and principle of your supply and it is impossible for you to have any need or desires unfulfilled. We project love and therefore our reality becomes love. Your reality is always a projection of your state of mind.

Our shadow is a good example to explain this as it actually works in exactly the same way. You are the creator of it and therefore automatically create it, but, if it wasn't for the light (God) it would not be possible.
Most people are always trying to change their projection, i.e. their reality, but they don't realize that their reality, like their shadow is only a projection of themselves and that you cannot change your projection without changing yourself. Work on yourself and your shadow will be what you want it to be. You cannot change your shadow if you don't first change yourself. Your shadow, future or reality can look any way you want it to look, just change yourself and it will automatically change.
You have to Be what you want to Be before you can live the reality you want to live.
You must look the way you want your shadow to look.

Finding God means finding the light. Most people always stand in the shadows and are afraid to come out into the light. They are afraid of what they might find if they started searching, and rightly so, it is quite a change. This requires absolute fearlessness and a lot of courage. But, it is only in the light that you get to project a shadow and create your reflection of who you really are.
Your reality becomes a reflection of you. If you stand in the darkness of unconsciousness, you just have to go with what is in the darkness, you have no control.

As long as you are in the light of consciousness you will always have a clear, solid shadow. It is only if you slip into the darkness (unconsciousness / absence of light) that your shadow becomes limited or faded. This is how your abundance becomes limited.
When we live in unconsciousness we just accept what happens around us and get thrown around all the time. This is because we are living in what has already been manifested by collective consciousness. We have no control because we are living in what is being created by our past, but when we are conscious we step into the new creation (what we have created) every second, so we get to choose what we want.

The shadow will be a shadow no matter what you do to make it a shadow or reflection. You can let go and stop trying to make a shadow (create abundance in your life). It will happen anyway. As long as you are in the light it will happen so just stand in it and let it shine through you.
When you realize that you are part of the light, then the light will always shine through you and when that happens you are fully in the flow or in consciousness. Step out of the illusion and concentrate on staying conscious because that is where your abundance lies.
Now is your opportunity to step out of the shadows and let the light work through you. We need to rise above all the belief systems and junk that has been programmed into our heads.

God is consciousness and is our only and constant supply of creation material. The knowledge that God is within us is our supply. Just being aware that the God-self within us is our source, Is our source and our abundance.
Just being conscious is our supply, so as soon as we slip out of consciousness or into the illusion our supply gets halted. We have to stay out of the illusion to be present in consciousness and to know that that is our supply. Consciousness is the only thing that is real. It is even the substance that this illusion is made from. There is no thing

in the illusion that can be our supply of abundance. Everything that comes through the illusion comes from God. The illusion (physical) is just a medium for God to pass us stuff through.
No Thing in the illusion can be your supply. Money is not your supply, it is just a tool, an effect of the supply. Your job, employer or salary is not your supply either, they too are just effects of the supply. No person, situation, business, etc can be your supply. If one of these other things were your supply you could easily become controlled by it.
If you see anyone other than God as your supply you are giving them the power to control you and you are the victim. You are letting them create a reality for you to step into.
If you depend on happiness, approval, love, security, etc from any person or object you will always be seeking. The only way to get it is through God consciousness. He is the substance that causes the effects.

"God can do for you only what God can do through you" - John Randolph Price.

Our whole purpose is to create because we are one with the creator and that is what he does. You are one with the source and since God has no limitations, neither do you.

Praying

There is no need to ask God for anything. There is no need to beg or plead or bargain with God. You are his child; abundance is your birth right.

Command the energy around you to create what you want and believe it will be so. Believing that it will happen is a vital part in manifesting. If you ask, beg and plead, you are acknowledging that you are not worthy of what it is you want and therefore it will not become a reality for you.
Command it out of authority, not egotistical authority but love authority by acknowledging and knowing that

substance works through you. Create it in God's name. Don't forget to do it with gratitude.

If your consciousness only goes as far as getting by, that is exactly how you will live. You don't need to "earn a living", you already have the right to live and everything is available for you. Just take it, it has already been given to you.
Seek ye the kingdom (wholeness) of God (which is consciousness) and the rest will be added unto you (you can have anything). "God's Kingdom" is substance, the stuff we use to manifest.
It is very important however to not only have this knowledge but to live it by ingraining it into your mind and truly seeing it in every situation. Live with love and gratitude.

The Bible speaks about the trinity of the Father, the Son and the Holy spirit. When you acknowledge all three and know what they really mean, that is God (consciousness). The Father is the creator, the Holy Spirit is the substance that we use for creation and the Son is the effect. That is the wholeness of God - substance, creation and effect.

God is not responsible for giving us stuff. He gives us himself, which is the substance to create these things with. If we pray to God for stuff, we are missing the point and denying the power he gave us.

Your attitude creates your reality

On the physical side of things it is important to understand what earth is made of and that everything is just energy. Everything is made up of different frequencies as we have discussed under "senses". There is no thing more real than any other thing. It is just a matter of what can be perceived by the tools or senses that you have.
Energy cannot be created or destroyed, it can only be changed. The same kind of energies will always stick together and attract energies that are similar to it. With

your mind you project thoughts and attitudes and since thought is energy, your thoughts are projected and create a certain impression. The process of thinking involves the movement of electrons in our brains. Even though this movement is tiny, it still affects other electrons around us.
The same kind of energies you project with your thoughts and actions will be in your experiences. This is explained very nicely by the fact that water turns into different crystals when being told "you fool" or "I love you". Even different music creates different crystals. This is a clear indication that our thoughts can create and affect everything around us, especially water and most things contain water.
That is why someone who is negative all the time will only experience more negativity. They create it. You create your own reality. Your attitude determines how your experiences are perceived.

Your mind is constantly creating what it is conscious of. You create what you believe you are so it is important therefore always to be conscious of what you are creating. The mind is very powerful. Thought is pure energy so it creates and transforms energy into matter. Every word moulds a certain state of matter.

You will still have certain experiences that are in your destiny but life can become much easier and smoother when you have a positive attitude. Resilience is another important factor in manifestation. We need to believe in a positive outcome, expect good things to happen and practice acceptance.

If you swear at the bus driver cutting you off every morning on your way to work you will upset your day and arrive stressed and angry. Can you see how your day will turn out? Stressed and angry. Now if you just ignore it and insist that nothing will ruin your day, you will arrive at work calm and happy and your whole day will proceed in

peace. The more we practice acceptance in all situations that are beyond our control, the smoother things will go. Success and happiness are determined not so much by what happens but rather by how we respond to it.
For as long as you consider yourself unfortunate (to be ill, poor, suffering, etc), you will be trapped in that because you keep creating it. If you keep thinking you are so poor and can't afford anything, that is exactly what your reality will be. An attitude like that does not inspire you to do anything about it. Some of the world's richest people come from the poorest background, just look at Oprah Winfrey for a good example.

Collective attitudes, which come from a group of people who are all in the same situation, also play some part in our environment. We can easily pull each other into a negative attitude or into a positive attitude. In a life-threatening situation your attitude can determine whether you survive or not.

Think highly of yourself and everyone around you. This is when everything in your life blossoms. When you think highly of others, you inspire them to live up to that because you believe in them. When you seek to have good done unto others, it is automatically drawn to you individually.

In order for the divine "I AM" energy to flow through you, you need to be yourself for a living no matter what actual work you do. If you try to be someone you are not, hate your job, and have to steal, cheat, lie and step on others to gain "success", you are blocking that energy. Love is that energy and when you are yourself you are relaxed, happy and joyful. When you are not being true to yourself, you are stressed, unhappy, depressed and no love can come through you. The key of all keys is love and gratitude. Everything you do must be about love.

As soon as you experience anything but love, love stops flowing through you and you are on your own, separated from consciousness and the flow of abundance.
Love is your supply and it is unlimited. You just have to tap into it. With love you can make anything happen. People respond better to love than to anger. Always stay in love and gratitude in order to stay in consciousness.

Putting intentions out

Many people think that all you need to do is will something and it will happen. This is not entirely accurate. You need to will something by having the willpower to make it happen and then you have to actually make it happen. Here is an example of how it works. When you want to pick up a glass you cannot just tell your arm to pick it up. You can sit there for days trying to will your arm to pick it up but it will not actually do it until you move the muscle and do it.
It is all about having a goal and working towards it. It is also useful to spend time and energy on making a collage book. In there you dedicate a page to each thing you want. Then cut out snippets and pictures of those things and paste them in the book. You can have a page for love, a page for where you want to live, a page for what job you want, a page for loosing weight, a page for having children, a page for becoming more conscious, etc. This will help you really focus on what you want and you will manifest it so much faster. I personally did this with the intention of having all these things within 5 years. I had every one within only one year!

As long as you stay in the sate of want, you can never have. As soon as you want something, that is denying that you already have it. This is the same concept as waiting for something that you already have. It is denying that you already have it and thereby delaying the process unnecessarily. You need to believe that you have it, and that it is on its way. It's just a matter of waiting a little bit.

That is why some people say that when you expect something, you push it away. This is confusing but it actually just means that if you don't go and get it, you will never reach it.
You must act as if you already have what you want and believe it because wanting it denies that you have it. Be at the Cause in the matter of how things change, rather than to being at the Effect of it. You don't have to sit back and wait for what life has to throw at you. Be the thrower!

What physical stuff can I create?

Our soul only wants what is best for us taking our karma and destiny into account. Therefore you will only get something if it is either involved in your destiny (lessons to learn) or if it will not interfere with that. That is why getting a Ferrari is quite difficult because it is an empty earthly wish that may inspire acts of the ego but if you wish for love or knowledge you will be given it. Only soul wishes are real wishes.

Don't however worry too much about what is your destiny and what you can or cannot have. As long as the intention behind it is right you probably can create it. The intention should be some higher purpose that is only in the best interest of everybody including the earth.
If your big dream is to make a lot of money from exporting wood from your local forest, it probably won't happen. There is no higher intention and you will be destroying the earth and creating a lot of lessons for yourself. You can have a dream to make money but make sure there is a good intention behind it and it doesn't cause any harm. If your dream is to live in the mountains to grow plants for medicine, that's great. You are helping the environment and playing a part in helping others.
If you pray for something that you want but it is not in your best interest, you simply won't get it. Rather pray for guidance and the ability to recognize when you are being guided so that you can find what you really want.

Rather than striving to fix things physically in our lives, strive for the consciousness to see reality through the illusion.

It is impossible to create from a place of unconsciousness. Trying to create from a place of greed, selfishness and disregard for others is trying to create in a place of unconsciousness and does not work. The only place we can create from is a place of consciousness, which harms nobody and serves love and gratitude.

Manifesting good health

If you want to heal something in your body or maintain good health, visualize your spirit as being perfect. Your body will reflect that. Stop believing that you are mortal and susceptible to all kinds of illnesses. You are immortal spirit and immune to everything. When you are in consciousness nothing can touch you.

In the case of illness in yourself and others, avoid focusing on the illness itself because if you do, you will be giving it power and acknowledging it. Once again you have to go through spirit to manifest. See the disease as unreal, it is part of the illusion and it has no power to sustain it. Spirit has no defects so disease does not exist. Do not focus on the illness, see only perfection. Acknowledge that there is nothing to heal.

Many illnesses are a belief of some sort. Beliefs can be inherited from your parents and manifest as illness (hereditary) but the soul has no beliefs. The soul can overcome that because it knows that is an illusion and illness is not real. Illness, even the ones we are born with are only obstacles or beliefs to overcome. There may be a lesson involved in having the illness but when you learn that lesson, be it humility or strength or whatever, you can overcome the effect that the illness has on you. If it is a permanent disability you can learn that you are not the body and stop being limited by it. Destiny and karma may have a lot to do with it too.

This does not mean you may not seek medical help to change the outcome of an illness. You are not the body and can heal it, even if doctors need to play a role. It is not the will of God for you to be sick and it is not the will of God for you to stay like that and accept it as your destiny or punishment. Sometimes medical intervention is the path to finding the freedom from the illness that invades you. Just be careful not to suppress symptoms in order to forget about an illness. The point is to make it go away or live with it knowing that it is not you, not to suppress it.

Eliminating what you don't want

Instead of just waiting for what you want; state what you want so you can clear away the stuff you don't.

This applies for anything that you want to change in your life. Take a good look at your life and decide what needs to be changed. It will only change if you make an active effort to change it.

The "belief in" is what creates "the manifestation of" so if you don't want something, stop believing in it. Stop believing that you do not deserve the best and that what you have is good enough. You need to stop believing that limitation, poverty, lack, etc exists. Believe that your life is perfect and it will become perfect.

When this is your state of being, how can you not succeed? You have succeeded already. It is not a question of whether you have what it takes but rather of whether you take what you have, and then use it.

Denying your ability to create your reality

When you say "I can't", you are giving your power away. It is won't, never is it can't. It is easier to deny your power than to own it because then you are responsible, nobody can feel sorry for you, and you must do something. We don't want to take responsibility for our choices because

there is always a chance of being ridiculed and told you are wrong.
Do not be disturbed by other people's influences, fears, beliefs, active memories or limitations.

Lack and limitations

LACK DOES NOT EXIST. There is no such thing. All there is, is everything, all around in saturated abundance. Really think about this for a second. God is unlimited.
It is very difficult for our limited minds to even imagine what unlimited or forever means. We have to create a picture in our heads for the mind to understand it and a picture needs a frame or box so that you can see it but "unlimited" or "forever" has no box or frame.
It is now time to release old belief systems that have been programmed into your mind. Let go of beliefs like, "money is limited", "my job is my source", "money means success", "without money I am worthless", etc.
You are the source of your supply so therefore it is unlimited and there is no way you can ever run out.
Most people fear not having enough but to fear lack means you believe in its existence and its power to rule you. Fear of lack creates lack. Focus on what you do have instead of what you don't. This will start eliminating your consciousness of lack.

Running into obstacles

If you are trying to manifest but still keep running into obstacles you will wonder if it is just part of the process or if you are being given a message that what you are trying to create, is not meant for you. To get the answer, go quiet in mediation and consider if it is something you are really determined to do or if it is just a road to get you somewhere else. Consider also if it is a selfish endeavor or if it is done with love and the purpose of helping others. That is normally a good indicator.

Manifesting negatively and doubting

The more conscious you become, the more instant your manifestation abilities take form. Some fear that they would accidentally create something bad just by thinking of the possibility of it happening. Creation happens through consciousness and therefore you can only create good things. When you are thinking negatively that is not consciousness so it cannot be created. A positive thought is hundreds of times more powerful than a negative one.
The spirit naturally creates and expresses abundance and this process can only be stopped by a belief in scarcity.
It is impossible to create nothing. Even mathematics shows us that zero multiplied by zero equals zero. Since it takes consciousness to create, you cannot create lack, you can only create abundance. Lack is illusion. Only the belief that lack does exist, exists.
Therefore creating nothing or lack is simply not creating at all. Creating lack is a handbrake for manifesting. All we need to do is release the belief of lack so the creative forces can flow.

The spirit flows through you (when you are being conscious) to reveal the reality of heaven on earth. Therefore you are the example of consciousness and nothing can go wrong with you. You are THEE example that nothing can go wrong so how can anything go wrong with you. If you are the example of being a perfect apple, how can you have a worm?

There are times when you will wonder, after trial and error whether it is all hogwash. That is a difficult stage because you are not yet able to stay in consciousness and still get pulled into the illusion often. You may also still find it difficult to differentiate between consciousness and illusion. This makes manifestation difficult too because you are so in and out of consciousness that it is not easy to be without doubt. Persevere and believe it, be the living proof that when done right, it does work.

You have to be able to stay out of the illusion before you can accept and know that that is all it is, an illusion. When you get through this phase and realize that it was only a phase, things will become easier. When something goes wrong even when you thought you were in consciousness, it is vital not to blame yourself or be disappointed in yourself, just work harder at staying in love. Blame and disappointment only pulls you back into the illusion.

God is the only cause. When we acknowledge limitations, we are limiting God and acknowledging a second cause (i.e. something else is responsible when things go bad). This second cause that you might be acknowledging is often referred to as Satan. There is no such thing. So release the power this belief has over you. You can't receive anything until you do this.
Therefore when we doubt, it is our own belief. Everything good is there; don't make up excuses not to take it. The only limitations we have are the ones we set for ourselves. Don't be a victim to circumstance, create your ideal reality.

Manifestation and living in the now

To create something, you need to visualize your dreams with every detail in place. Paint the picture fully and believe that you will have it. It is not just a dream; it is your reality right now in the making. No dream is unachievable; don't let anyone convince you otherwise. The time from now and when it actually happens is in direct proportion to you being able to see yourself there now. Now go and make it happen, it won't just appear out of thin air.
You have to affirm and accept it as if it has already happened. If you can accept that you are beautiful or rich or wise or whatever, then you will be.
Your creation will follow the clearest picture in your mind. Therefore it is very important to keep recreating your dreams and focus on them. If your doubt is stronger than your dream, the doubt will manifest.
You need to see yourself doing it. It can't be in the future or even a second away. You have to not imagine it but

actually see it happening right now. Then you have to believe it one hundred percent without a single doubt.

Spiritual arrogance

This is often the biggest blockage to manifestation. Spiritual arrogance is when you think you are better than others and take credit for what you know or have.
Spiritual arrogance can lead to a closed and opinionated mind. It can lead you to think that whoever doesn't do what you do is wrong. This is often the case with people who are newly vegetarian or have decided not to drink alcohol. They tend to judge everyone who is not and try to convince others to be like them.

A part of becoming more conscious is to realize that all are equal and to eliminate all judgment. Yet, as we learn more about behaviour, the truth and the method to manifesting our best reality, it is rather easy to slip into a feeling of superiority and judgment. This only gets the ego involved and shuts off the flow of love, which shuts off your abilities.
When we think we know better than someone else, we are judging them and that is pride. When we love someone, we acknowledge equality and recognize the God in them. Even if others do not see things the way you might, they are the same as you but choose a different reality. That is what they choose!!!

There are also many religions and spiritual groups who believe that they are the "chosen ones" and that only they have been especially selected by God to be superior or entitled to certain privileges. There is no such thing as the "chosen ones". It is rather the "choosing ones". The opportunity is open to everyone but only a few choose to take it at this time. When the rest are ready, they too will choose to know.

As soon as you think you are involved in the pouring of consciousness through you, you stop the flow. You need to step aside for it to flow. We are not the doer but rather the allower - the person who lets substance work through him. This does not make us better in any way. There is no competition and everybody is on their own quest. Nobody else's quest or level is any of our business. Being in arrogance is once again being in the illusion and stops the flow because consciousness has no concept of self, only of all being one.

It is important to remember that it is not our doing, we are just the channel. Just as a ray cannot exist and shine light without the sun, we cannot be conscious and shine light on others without God. Therefore it is not us doing anything, but merely being an expression of God. When we loose gratitude, we loose power. When we are a ray denying the sun's power, we loose our ability to shine light and warmth on the rest of the world. We have to completely surrender our lives to being that ray. As soon as we think it is us, we deny our connection to the sun which puts us at risk of fading and disappearing.
Spiritual pride puts an absolute stop in your manifestation abilities (which are not yours, but God's).

Rather than teaching others from a position of superiority, we can share with others from a level of love and equality. The secret is to do it with love, not with pride. Be careful not to perceive oneself as right, which makes others wrong. Know that you always have more to learn and as your consciousness expands, you will find that what you believed was absolutely right, is now not so accurate anymore. Even this book may not be completely accurate even though in my consciousness at this time, according to my experience I believe it to be.

Manipulation

If you ever use mind power or psychology consciousness to get anyone to do anything, it will backfire on you because you are influencing them. If you use your knowledge to gain something and hurt someone else in the process, even in a small way (like trying to get something cheaper), this is not acting in love and creates karma. Chances are it won't work anyway because you are not in consciousness when attempting it. You will find that if you are in consciousness, you will automatically be led to the bargains or circumstances will be to your advantage. You can have, do and be anything you want as long as it does not hurt anyone else.

Helping others

As the excitement of learning and realizing the truth engulfs us we feel the need to tell anyone and everyone about our new discoveries only to come to the realization that nobody wants to know. You may even be called crazy or depressed by your friends and family because they don't understand the change. Many people will not understand the difference between what you are telling them and religion and may think you have become a "happy clapper" and are trying to preach to them.

The most important thing in helping others is to be yourself. You can only be useful in the world if you can relate to others and they see you as an equal. Also, wait for them to ask. People don't want to be preached to. It is human nature to resist being told what to do and to take advice when it is not asked for. Becoming conscious is a path for the seeker. You have to seek it. You have to want to have it.

People who are really conscious don't advertise it. You have to be really guided to come across one. The only way to change people is through being an example of pure love, not through persuasion.

When trying to force beliefs or knowledge onto anyone, you are apposing their free will and going against the principles of freedom and love which is consciousness. So in the very act of trying to convince them, you are teaching them the opposite of what you are trying to explain.

Stress and worry

Don't let stress get you down, you need to go about creating your dream with ease and confidence. Stress and worry kills the creative force because it automatically takes you out of consciousness and therefore out of the flow. It is the same principle as folding a water pipe, it makes the water stop flowing. More pressure - less flow, less pressure - more flow.

The only single way to create is to stay in the love dimension and not be pulled out of it by negative emotions. That is why the key to being conscious is to sort your emotions out first.

You might have heard that one must create your reality but not be attached to what you want because if you hold onto it, you won't get it. This is because when you manifest something you must acknowledge that you will have it but at the same time you mustn't care if you get it or not. This is simply because worrying about it will stop the energy from flowing, you have to just trust and know that it will all work out.

What should I focus on when attempting to manifest?

When attempting to manifest something you really want, it is important to focus on the end result and act as if it has already happened. Do not focus on how it is going to happen or on the physical outcome. Focus on the feeling you would have if you already had that outcome. To make this easier pretend that it already happened 5 years ago and it is old news already.

So if you want a new home, do not focus on how you are going to get it or on the fact that you cannot afford it. Focus on the picture and the feeling of having it already. Imagine yourself sitting in your new lounge, in front of the fireplace that you wanted. Feel the warmth, smell the fragrance of the house, see the colours of your furniture and feel the comfort of having everything you desire.

If you focus on how it is going to happen, you are controlling it and thereby stopping the natural process. Abundance does not come from any earthly source. There has to be something behind whatever you think your earthly source is. A physical source is just the visible effect. If you are in the illusion then you have to be in control but when you are in consciousness, God is in control and you can relax.

Spirit (God) is abundant, we just have to remember and realize it. You have to let go and let the universe take care of it. If you try to control too much the real creativity or abundance cannot flow because you keep putting logs in the river. Flow with the river.

Learning to receive

One often hears spiritual people telling each other that they must learn to receive. Learning to receive is not about learning to receive stuff or money. It is about knowing or acknowledging that you have the ability to manifest. That you can create what you want. It is about accepting the worthiness of being a part of God, not the worthiness of having stuff.
Once you get that right, learning to receive is learning to accept the things you want. It is no use asking the universe for something and then carrying on believing that you don't have it. This is the final part of manifestation. After you have asked, believe that you already have it. That is receiving. You always receive as much as you can accept.

Tests

Every time we learn something new or learn another way of staying out of the illusion, we get tested to see if we have learned the lesson. This also helps us to strengthen that ability. For example: You may have just learned that your day depends on your attitude so you go around being friendly and loving to everyone. The first few days you may find that everything is against you and everybody else is in a bad mood.

This is your test to see if you can really do it and to help you practice to keep doing it.
Once you have mastered the manifestation and consciousness thing you may still find that occasionally things still go wrong. It is not about what happens but rather about how you deal with it. You will also see how these things often get sorted out in the most miraculous way as if the universe planned it just for you and that you are so looked after.

Willpower

Willpower plays a huge role in manifestation. It is the "doing it" part of manifestation. We have explored the spiritual side, the physical side and now the "making it all happen" side. We have discussed how you cannot just wait for something to happen, you have to actually do something about it. So say you want to manifest a financially free life with no limitations. You are managing to stay in consciousness most of the time and you are being given a lot of business ideas and opportunities. On the physical side everything is sorted too. You have the resources and you know exactly what to do. Now you have to use willpower to make it all come together. The business is not just going to run itself, you have to make it happen and work toward a goal. When you absolutely make up your mind to do something, that is manifestation in motion. Willpower needs to be very strong to be able to follow through with anything.

You need to test and strengthen your willpower by doing things like becoming vegetarian for 6 months, or stopping smoking, or avoiding chocolate for a while. This will help you to manifest things by willing to succeed. If you cannot do a short willpower, how can you succeed in any endeavor in your life? You won't have enough willpower to make it happen. Once you have decided to do something you cannot break it because that will show that your willpower is very weak. This is a really powerful tool to have.

When you strive for success in any situation, you are practicing willpower, which will help you to manifest success. In everything you do, you will be trying for the best, because you always want to be successful. That is how willpower creates manifestation.

We can see easily how water responds to our will by looking at the water crystals formed by intentions. Clouds are water in the gas state so it responds especially easily to our will. You can even make a cloud disappear. Just send your energy out then use past tense to say the cloud has disappeared and thank the energy. This is a bit of a waste of energy but may help convince you how strong your willpower really is.

The will of God is what you are. You are part of God, therefore his will is your will. We have been taught to be fearful of God's will but all God wants is for you to know that you are one with him and use that power wisely.

When we use all the secrets of the universe, we can make a huge success of anything. You will be amazed how anything you do turns out to be successful. When you persist, refusing to accept failure, the object of your will must be materialized.

Whatever you want to achieve, surround yourself by people who will enforce the belief that you can. People who tell you that you can't will only destroy your willpower.

Money

Most of us have at the very least, some stress about money, be it too little or too much and trying to hold onto it.

Once again, as with manifesting anything else the secret is non-attachment. When you are in consciousness all the time, money flows automatically. When you get attached to it, you are worrying about it and that once again kills the

flow. If you are doing God's work, you must know he will be looking after you at all times.
There is nothing wrong with wanting material things, just don't depend on it. It is here to enjoy but don't get attached.
"What you sow, you shall reap". The whole concept of giving has nothing to do with giving the church your 10% tithing or any material giving. It is not about the harder you work the more money you will get, or about giving everything away and then God will look after you. It is about giving of yourself, giving love and acceptance. It is about giving consciousness.

Being abundant has nothing to do with money. Money is just the by-product. It is not what you should strive for. If you strive for consciousness, happiness and love, money will come automatically.
Money is only a medium, it is not the actual stuff we need. What we need is an abundance consciousness so that there is never any shortage of anything. Your wealth is not measured by your amount of money but rather by your ability to create it.
Money is not what we should be focusing on. It is just the by-product of being in consciousness. Focusing on the by-product (money) does not create the product (the outcome you want) for you.
God is the source of all your abundance. Abundance is the joy you get from being fulfilled and only God or the knowledge of knowing that God is everything, can give you that joy. The joy itself is what God is made of and what our souls are made of so therefore God is the source of all our abundance. Without God you will feel empty and lost. Money is a by-product of happiness, fulfillment and joy, which is God.

How do I stop worrying about it?

Most people's biggest worry that prevents them from living peacefully is money and it is the easiest one to eliminate. We have this idea in our heads that as soon as we have that car or a bigger house or whatever, then we will be happy. You now know that happiness is not created by things, it is a state of being and all else will come with that. So stop believing that things will make you happy and then stop taking out loans to pay for them. The less debt you have, the freer you can be.

See money simply as a tool that allows you to be free. Money gives us freedom of choice - to travel, play, create and grow. The goal is not to have money but rather to live the life you want and live to be yourself. Money gives you the freedom to do that. Go where you want, live where you want, live the lifestyle you want, etc. It is the physical side of manifesting. The problem is that most people focus too much on the money. Just trust that your needs will be provided for. You can even take money completely out of the equation. Just focus on what you want to create and let the universe sort out the money side. Sometimes you may even find that the universe makes you wait till minutes before the rent is due but if you stay in consciousness, you will always be looked after. As long as you are focusing on money, you will live in insecurity and waiting.

Release your restrictions about money, if you are going to be yourself, it automatically has to be a part of you, don't be scared of it. Source will always provide enough.

Fear of money

Everybody wants it but most people are actually terrified of having it on a subconscious level. If you didn't have money and now you suddenly do, it would create a huge amount of stress trying to hold onto it. It would also mean that now you no longer have all the excuses for why your life is the way it is. You may even loose friends or gain some false friends in the process and you no longer know who to trust.

Many people believe that to have money is a bad thing and makes one a bad person. Money is not a bad thing but getting it from being power and material orientated and doing anything to anybody to get money is obviously not a good thing. One does not have to walk over others or be selfish in order to be rich, actually quite the opposite is true.

Then there is also the worthiness part of it. Most people don't actually think they are worthy of having what they really want. People set themselves a certain standard by putting themselves in a certain league. This can be determined by the way they are brought up or by their first salary. They simply exclude certain things from their reality and decide it is not in their league, like for example satellite television or expensive shoes. They don't even look at these items in the store because they have denied the possibility that it will ever be a part of their lives. That is why they are always stuck in that rut. You create your own reality and if you are forever denying things out of it, you will continue to create lack. You have to see the world as all yours, everything is available to you. You just have to know that to make it happen. You deserve everything. You deserve the best.

This does not mean you must be careless with the money you have, just start seeing a bigger reality for yourself and work on making it happen. Stop settling for an average salary. Stop settling for an average life. The sense of being powerless repels abundance so don't wait for money to make you powerful, be powerful and you will automatically make money.

Money problems are the average adult's boogieman. When you were a kid the boogieman in the cupboard was very scary but as you got older you realized it didn't exist but your belief and therefore fear of him made all the difference. That is the same way something can only scare you if you believe it is real. If a money problem comes along, or any other problem for that mater, just recognize that it is not real. It is part of the illusion, only God / good is real. God is everything, including this meaningless problem, so therefore it will be sorted out.

Running toward more money out of fear of having no money keeps you in fear and frustration. The goal is not worth the suffering.

Running a business consciously

This is not always the easiest thing to do especially since stress, staff problems, time factors, cash flow and many other things are in your face all the time. It is however, very important to run it as consciously as you can if you are going to really make it work. In business you have to be brave, even fearless and trust the universe. Opportunities in life come by creation, you have to take a chance. Don't look for a gold mine, create one.

In order to succeed in anything especially in business, you have to be hungry for success. You have to be 100% determined to be successful and create it. You need super strong willpower and visualize it only being successful. Even though doubts may come in, try very hard not to dwell on them and reassure yourself that you are being looked after. Even if the business ends up taking you somewhere else, it was still meant to be that way and may just be a path to something better.
Always keep in mind that true success is not about how much money you make but rather comes about when you are doing what you want to be doing in every aspect.

How you handle your staff is almost more important that anything else in business. This is a true reflection of your consciousness. Always remember that you are dealing with human beings and that they also have opinions, self worth, likes and dislikes, etc. It is easy to force a person into a certain job role and make them do it because you are paying them but if you fit a job into a person your business will be much more successful. So as an example; if you have a cleaner who is very slow, you can send her on her way or you can find out from her what is going on. She may tell you that she is allergic to dust. Now you can either say "well, you are the cleaner and sweeping is your job" or you can work out something where she takes on some other duties and a different person does the sweeping. This way your staff will be much happier and since staff run a business, your business will be much more successful.

If you employ somebody and drive him or her away from their family by over working them and restricting them in themselves, you are not being very conscious either. Treat your staff as you would like to be treated and they will be hard working, honest and loyal.

Relationships

Life is all about relationships. We have a relationship with every person who crosses our path. You have a relationship with your parents, your children, your colleagues, the salesman at the store and even the guy begging for money at the traffic light. In every relationship you act a certain way and the other person acts a certain way and there are at least ten different ways you can relate depending on your and the other person's beliefs, expectations, masks, labels, etc. We get given the experience of relationships to point out these things about ourselves to us so that we can improve and grow. If you are stuck on a certain lesson and struggling to learn it, you will be given opportunities by all kinds of people to learn that same lesson. For example if you need to learn how not to get irritated you will be irritated by the slow shopkeeper, the traffic in front of you, your husbands silliness and maybe even your dog jumping on the furniture. These opportunities will keep presenting themselves through other people until you learn from them.

It is all about how you handle situations. Without relationships there would be nothing to compare yourself to, nothing to learn and no way of finding out who you are or are not. The only way to get to know yourself is with others as they will show you if you are acting in love or not by their responses to your words and actions.

Karmic relationships

A karmic relationship is formed when two people have contracted to help each other with a certain lesson or they are returning a lesson that has played out in a previous life. Often the abuser will become the abused, the killer becomes the killed, the manipulator becomes manipulated and the cheater gets cheated on. In a romantic setting these relationships are often driven by lust or fear more than love. If the lesson is not learned in that relationship, it will be repeated in the next. When you find that one relationship turns out just like the previous one did, it is normally a good sign that it was a karmic relationship and if you still have not learned the lesson it will only be repeated again.

In a karmic relationship you will always create what you need (according to your beliefs). If you want to meet your ideal partner, you will meet someone who will fulfill your needs at that consciousness, which will probably be money, sex, etc but when you are on a higher consciousness your ideal partner will be someone completely different and the main need that you will need to have fulfilled is that this partner will share seeking the spiritual path with you and growing together.
That is why certain relationships expire. People outgrow each other's consciousness. The one will move forward and the other will stay behind and they will not meet each other's needs anymore.

Relationship Dymanics

Human beings need recognition and affection and a loving relationship provides these basic needs.

The dynamics of a relationship has very much to do with one's self worth and security within oneself. Insecurities within oneself is probably the biggest factor in relationship problems.

Every person has needs within a relationship and some are legitimate and others are not. If we had no needs, we would not bother to have a relationship in the first place.

Legitimate needs in a relationship:
People who have a healthy "self concept" expect emotional support and understanding, companionship and sexual sharing from their partner. They do not expect their partner to make them feel loveable or worthwhile. They have loved ones to enrich their lives.

Illegitimate needs:
An illegitimate need is when one needs someone else to convince you, you are worthy and borrow security from others.

It is important not to confuse self love with selfishness. Self love enhances one's ability to love others and selfishness / narcissism is concerned only with oneself and doesn't care about others.

The keys to a successful relationship are self love, interdependence, acceptance and empathy.

There are 3 basic types of relationships regarding dependency:
1) Dependant - parties lean on each other and one falls when the other is not there. Martyr manipulator relationships are normally dependent relationships.
2) Independent - each party stands alone and they connect very little. They don't know much about the other's life and basically live separately under the same roof.
3) Interdependent - if one lets go the other feels loss but recovers balance. Both have good self esteem but experience deep love and connection. In an interdependent relationship, intimate information is shared, both parties are able to be emotionally vulnerable, habits are developed that involve both partners, and both parties emotional needs are fulfilled.

In the ideal relationship, parties have separate identities but being together and sharing are intensely enjoyable and important. This does not mean there is no conflict but when there is, both parties want to resolve it quickly so that they can go back to their relationship that means so much to them both.

There are 6 basic types of couple relationships dynamics:

1) Passionate love (lust relationship)
   These relationships are based purely on lust and generally don't last very long. They can be very erratic and have very high highs and very low lows.

2) Familiar love (comfort zone)
   These people have known one another for a long time and find it difficult to live without each other. They cannot imagine a life without the other and will rather suffer unhappiness than be without the other.

3) Pragmatic love (purpose relationship)
   These relationships are held together by some kind of purpose. This purpose could be a business, or children or even money related.

4) Altruistic love (mothering, self sacrifice)
   Some people have a need to mother or give of themselves and sometimes a relationship can fulfill that need. There will be a definite parent / child relationship dynamic in this kind of couple relationship. This can be detrimental to the one being "mothered" as it prohibits them from being independent and self sufficient, leaving them helpless when the "mother" is no longer there.

5) Love play (sexual, meaningless)
   This is slightly different to passionate love relationships in the sense that this is normally a one night stand and there is no sense of needing or depending on the other person in any kind of long term fashion.

6) Possessive love (possessive, moody, jealous)
   This is probably the most dangerous type of relationship dynamic. The one partner will be totally controlled by the other and loose all sense

> of self worth and independence. They will fear leaving the relationship for what the other might do if they were to leave or they are made to believe that they are nothing without the other and choose to stay.

We tend to create the same kind of relationships over and over until we learn to recognize the pattern or the type of dynamic we set up every time. These relationships are all damaging in one sense or another. Only when we recognize our patterns can we move on from them and work towards becoming ready for a constructive relationship.

Fairy tale relationships

Fairy tale relationships are hard to come by. This is the kind of relationship every person dreams about. The dream is that one day you will meet your soulmate whom you have been with for many lifetimes and there will be fireworks when you find each other again. Then you have a long lasting, perfect, happy marriage and everybody lives happily ever after. The End.

There is no relationship that does not take effort and dedication to make it work. Even if it is all fireworks and fairy tales, there will still be work involved in making it stay that way.

Constructive relationships

This is when two whole people have found each other and are not trying to complete themselves by depending on the other. They grow together and do not try to hinder each other's growth in any way. They still have their arguments but try to find a suitable solution where nobody gets hurt and always consider the other's feelings and views. They are by no means dependant on each other, fearful of each other or needy of each other and both strive to live as consciously as possible. They communicate in a way that builds each other up and never break each other down in any way. They never compromise who they are to fit with someone else.

How to prepare for a constructive relationship

The most important thing to do is to find yourself first. You have to be completely happy and comfortable with yourself and not need anybody to complete you. A relationship is about sharing completion, not finding it. It's about sharing joy and happiness, not finding it. If you are not happy going into a relationship, you will have no happiness to put there.

When you know who you are, you will automatically attract the right person to you and it will be easier to recognize when you have found your soulmate because there are no games involved when you are both secure in who you are. You will also realize that it is not about just finding anybody who will be compatible with you, it is about finding your soul mate and they too will be comfortable with themselves and not need you to fill a gap they cannot fill themselves.

Many relationships are based on neediness, a need to control, a need to possess, lust, a need for acceptance, or co dependency. It is common to fall into an "I'll love you if you love me" contract.

A constructive relationship is about being yourself with someone.

Our picture of what the perfect relationship should look like is normally based on memories and belief systems. We have beliefs around age, race, income, career, etc. Ideally we should love someone for who they are with no expectations of who they should be. If you can both be comfortable with who the other is, great. If not, you both still have things to work on or maybe the contract has expired. If you feel the contract has expired and there are no more lessons, then leave in love and let the other be. The ideal relationship involves both partners bringing each other up and encouraging each other to become everything they can be.

To recognize a building relationship from a breaking one is easy. In the building one you will feel content, happy and fulfilled and in the needy one there will be in suffering and pain. If you are in a destructive relationship you need to be very honest with yourself to assess your beliefs and issues because you are most likely stuck in a certain relationship dynamic that can only be broken when you recognize the pattern. You need to be very honest with yourself and asses weather this is a lesson you must learn or if you have already learned it and it is time to move on. If you just leave without fixing your patterns, your next relationship will only turn out the same.

Common relationship problems

Control

Control is a very necessary part of living in this world but when we become obsessed with it and control other people it can become very destructive. Controlling another person does not allow them to grow and express themselves. It stunts their growth and their self worth.

It is vital to assess your beliefs and active memories around the need to control everything. It could be that you had no control as a child and the unpredictability of life was terrifying. Maybe if you can predict what will happen, you think that you will never get hurt.

Communication

Communication consists of a sender, a receiver and a message. A message is sent not only using words but also through facial expressions, gestures, body language, and tone of voice. Words is only 7%

Communication is a very common problem in relationships because most people don't know how to express what they are feeling without attacking the other or saying something in a hurtful way. It is important to stop in a situation and take your attention off the situation and rather assess why it is such an issue for you. Look at what

belief is kicking in. Focus on finding the problem in yourself, not in the other person. Then think of a nice way to address it, if it still needs to be addressed and take the other person's feelings into consideration. If you had to hear what you are about to say from someone else, how would you want to hear it? When you start talking something out, without any defense mechanisms in place, you will most often find there was no problem to begin with, only a misunderstanding.
It is in the nature of the mind to ever expand. That is why looking at a view makes us feel free and sitting in an office makes us feel stifled. The same principle goes for communication. When we communicate and discuss we are opening the mind and letting it flow. When we attack or fight we are blocking the mind, which only leads to frustration. Communication ends separation. Attack promotes it.

All emotions create either a feeling of comfort or of discomfort. Every choice you make is based on whether you think the outcome will bring you comfort or discomfort. What you want to eat, what car to buy, where you live, what job you do, etc. All the choices you have made in your life are based on this. Sometimes we sacrifice immediate comfort for long term comfort as in the case of exercise or diet.
Yet it is never the actual experience that brings you comfort or discomfort but rather your interpretation of it based on beliefs and active memories. For example, a trip to the ocean may be great for one person where the wind, sand and humidity may be an irritation for someone else.
Essentially these emotions of comfort and discomfort are based on our needs. If our needs are being met, we feel comfort. If not, discomfort is felt. Therefore positive emotions are felt when our needs are being met and negative emotions arise when something is against our needs.

The more you can express your needs, the more likely it is that your needs will be met and you will experience positive emotions rather than negative ones.
When you are feeling a negative emotion consider for a moment:
What button is being pushed?
What emotion am I feeling?
What do I need that I am not receiving?
What is my pay off for not getting what I want?

Very often our unhappiness is measured and increased by our inability to express ourselves.
When you know what you want and who you are, what you accept and what you don't accept, you become responsive instead of reactive and your relationship with everyone has to change.
This does not necessarily mean that anyone else will change (although they could). It simply puts your power back in your hands.

Here are some general rules to getting your message across without conflict:
Say what you feel so that the attention is on yourself, not on the other person which may have caused defensiveness.
So if you say "You did ...", the other person will immediately get defensive but if you say "I feel rejected when you ...", it takes the attack out of the sentence.
Never word it in such a way that you make the other person feel guilty or responsible, that is manipulation.
The idea is to express your needs and accept responsibility for your beliefs and active memories. For example, "when you drove recklessly I felt unsafe and afraid", rather than "you drive like an idiot, do you want to kill us?"
This way you are not attacking and the other person will not be defending, they are simply being given an opportunity to understand you better and it will be more likely that your needs will be met.
Here is a list of words you could use to express yourself better:

Anxious, afraid, bitter, resentful, angry, confused, discouraged, empty, frustrated, guilty, helpless, invisible, jealous, lonely, left out, insecure, mad, sorry, withdrawn, sad, hurt.

Respond instead of reacting. When you feel attacked, the immediate reaction is to defend or attack back. By responding in a calm manner, one can quickly defuse a situation and not get involved. The moment you try to defend yourself, you are seeking approval and you are giving the other person power over you.
You could use phrases like:
"I'm sure you see it that way"
"Name calling and shouting won't get us anywhere"
"I'm not willing to accept your labels"
"This is a good example of why we need to discuss this issue"
"It's not ok for you to speak to me that way"
"You agreed to hear me out"
"Let's do this some time when we are calmer"
"Its interesting that you see it that way"
"I'm sorry you are upset"
"I'm sorry you don't approve"
"Would you like to try and say that in a way that is assertive and not aggressive?"

Allow each person to have their say without being interrupted and listen while the other is speaking. Remember that this person thinks that they are as right as you think you are and that you are both trying to force the other one to see your point of view.

Do not shout, even if you feel the other person is not listening.
Some people have a belief that intense emotions are needed to keep a relationship alive, or you have to scream and shout to show that you are in control or you have to always be right else you are inferior or failing in some way.

Rather call a time out and write what you need to say in a letter. Another way is to have a box where both parties can insert cards on which is written what they would like to discuss. The cards can then be taken out and discussed one by one in a calm environment.

Never assassinate anyone's character. There is nothing that anyone can do that validates being called names and being made to feel unworthy. Just because somebody does not agree with you, does not mean they need to be ripped apart. This kind of desperation to get someone to agree with you never works.

Don't make assumptions on what the other person has done or about what they are feeling. Hear them out.

Don't give advice where it is not asked for. Nobody likes being helped when they don't think they need it.

Don't expect someone else to change. If they want to deal with their issues, it is up to them. One cannot make anyone do that.

It is best to express anger at the time of an event rather than storing it. Stored anger often becomes passive aggression and translates into other problems like over eating, boredom, depression, physical illness, smoking, drinking or other addictions or it gets expressed in sarcasm, nit picking, gossiping or irritability.

The trick is to be assertive , not aggressive, knowing who you are and not trying to mask an insecurity. Assertive behaviour does not include the need to win or compete where aggressive behaviour does.
Aggression seeks not only to state one's point of view but also to attack the other's point of view.

Be careful not to use labels. When you label someone it does not matter if your observation is accurate or not, it

rarely increases the likeliness that your needs will be met. When you judge or categorize you are more susceptible to rejection, which makes your chances of that person giving you what you want even less.
Demands decrease your chances of needs being met where requests increase them. Asking someone to change / think / feel / believe a certain thing or in a certain way is not going to help you. Establish what it is you really need. If you need attention don't ask your partner to work less or love you more. Rather ask for specifics like going out for a romantic dinner. When this is not possible try suggesting something different later, or open a date up for discussion. You can say that you miss your partner and would really like some value time. Avoid saying things like "you're always so busy, you don't care about me anymore"

There will be many times when your needs still don't get met, even with good communication skills. It is unrealistic to expect that you will never experience negative emotions but by using the tools provided you can recognize your own issues and move on much faster.
You will notice that when you use manipulation or ill intentions to do something it rarely works out for you. If you do it the right way with integrity and trust it automatically falls into place.

According to research, the greater the self disclosure within a relationship, the greater the marital happiness becomes. In other words, the more you communicate about your feelings and where you're at in any situation, the happier and more connected you will feel to your partner.

A good way to instill good communication every day is to start your and your partner's day with something like "good morning beautiful / the love of my life / whatever" instead of "get up, you're going to be late". The way you wake up in the morning can easily determine the rest of your day and the first relations you have with one another can determine the communication between you for the rest of the day and eventually for the rest of your relationship.

Victim / Martyr

In many relationships one person ends up taking the role of the martyr and the other the victim. Either party can take either of these roles. It is a relationship flaw that gradually becomes stronger as it is reinforced. If you see each other as equals and maintain the respect of being each other's soul mates, this will not happen. If it has already you need to have a good look at yourself and determine why you feel inferior and allow yourself to be the victim or why you feel superior and allow yourself to be the martyr by not taking your partner's view into consideration.

The victim normally has a weak self esteem and believes that they are worthless without the other. Remember that nobody is better than you are and you certainly do not need anyone. If you choose to be with someone it should be a choice out of love, not from neediness or lack of self worth.

The martyr normally also has a weak self esteem, as ironic as it sounds. They are normally trying to prove their own strength, which they don't know they already have, by belittling someone else. It makes them feel strong and powerful to see someone else being weak. They can do this with various tools including physical abuse, emotional abuse or manipulation.

In some cases the roles seem to be a certain way when in fact they are reversed. For example, a woman might pretend to be the victim by always complaining about her husband when in fact she uses that very tool to manipulate him, making him the victim. She will forever be telling him how terrible he is and making him feel guilty. People who do this often use tears to get what they want.

In any type of abusive relationship one's unworthiness gets affirmed daily and after a while you believe it so much that you almost need to be reminded of it. Being rejected by the abuser is sometimes the hardest part of it all. It's as if one is sad that they will no longer be there to believe in your unworthiness anymore. As whacked as it sounds, the abused person's biggest fear is often being rejected by the abuser.

One wants to grow spiritually and the other doesn't

When one partner wants to grow spiritually and the other doesn't, a tricky situation is created especially when neither were very interested before. The problem comes in where the one that is working on improving themselves expects the other to do the same. The other partner may become jealous and fearful at this new idea coming between them and changing everything. The one that is not interested should never be forced because that will create instant resistance. The best thing to do is just to carry on and live by example, meaning to be the best you can be, but not try to prove yourself to be more important. Often in this kind of relationships the parties eventually outgrow each other if they do not grow together.

Your attitude about your relationship determines a lot about it. Concentrate on the good aspects of your partner, not the bad and see the unity, not the differences. If you were the same you wouldn't fit together, like a puzzle. You need to always see yourselves as equals and as an addition to yourself, only making you better.

Love

The concept of love is very often confused. Neediness, compassion, lust and many other things have been called love, even fear. These are the types of situations that can be associated with pain, disappointment, excitement and all kinds of other active memories.

Love is in fact not an emotion but rather the feeling when no other emotions suppress it. Love is never given to you, it is only felt by you. It is the substance, which is God, pure consciousness. When you are conscious of love being around you, you can tap into it. When you allow yourself to feel it, there is instant happiness. It is there all the time but can easily be blocked by negativity.

Love is the feeling you get when you are in nature. When you can see the beauty and be grateful for everything and everyone, then you are living in love.
There is beauty and therefore love in everything, it's just a matter of being open to seeing it. The same concept goes for people. When you are open to seeing the beauty and good in every person, you will feel love for them.

Obviously there are certain people that you care for more than others and therefore you say you love them more. There is love for your partner, your dog, your child, etc.
This is only because you see more good and beauty in them than in others. The rest of the equation depends on lust, neediness, compassion, preference, compatibility and many other factors. These factors can all be part of why you "love" a person but they should be recognized for what they are and not just be labeled as "love".

The most important factor in living a life of love is to allow yourself to be loved. If you cannot feel the love of God in yourself, you cannot feel it in others. It is there already; you only need to allow yourself to feel it. If you cannot love yourself, you cannot love anything or anyone. Once again, loving yourself is a confidence thing not an arrogance thing. Acknowledging who you really are instills love for yourself, denial of that and trying to be something you are not, instills arrogance.

God gave us the ability to love not for the sake of the person that we love but for ourselves, for the sake of our soul. When we feel love we are reminded of who we really are and how great it is to experience life.

Loving involves committing oneself to accepting others; something only those who accept themselves can do.

Sex

Sex is an energy exchange between two people. It has the potential to be a beautiful sharing of yourself with someone special or it can be an attempt at seeking instant gratification and thereby happiness.
It is important not to confuse lust for love. Love is real and long term and is felt in the heart; where lust is felt you know where and dies after a very short while. Lust is often an empty feeling where you need to fill something that is lacking in yourself where love is a more fulfilled, long term feeling.

With the understanding of real love one would never want to experience sex with anybody who does not desire that experience with them, is not mature enough or old enough to know if they want to and do not have integrity around that.
Just as emotions are chemicals in the body and you can get addicted to them, so is sex a chemical and you can get addicted to it. It can make you loose perspective and only see what you want to see. Lust is blind!

There are so many mixed signals around sex in society. It is advertised as something that gives us the most pleasurable experiences that there is and also as one of the most necessary things in life. We base our life, our self worth and our entire lives on "who will sleep with me" and how sexy I am.
We often see women advertise sex, when they want love and men advertise love when they want sex. Men in society have been taught that sex comes first and then love will grow from that. Women see love first and sex comes later as an expression of love. This is not really a men or women thing, it is more a consciousness thing and it happens that women are generally more conscious about relationships and love than men because in society, women are generally permitted to feel more.

Conscious parent and child relationships

One of your most important relationships in your life is the one you have with your parents. Children are extremely susceptible to picking up beliefs and active memories and the ones they pick up during childhood are often the most significant ones that they will carry through life with them. It is unfortunate that children do not come with manuals but lucky for us there is a lot of literature available to this generation on how to be a good parent. As a parent you can only do your best and even the best parents' children still pick up some baggage, it is part of that soul's lesson to overcome them so don't blame yourself as a parent, just do your best. It all happens as it should.

The world is a big, scary place for a child and their single biggest need is security, not money or the latest toys or even the best university. It is up to you as a parent to provide them with that security and make them feel safe in their environment. When a child is allowed to run the household and the parents are afraid of it, the child becomes impossible because it has so much fear. It is important for a child to know that the parents are in control and that they do not have to take on that responsibility. Consistency, routine and discipline are the key factors to creating security for a child. They want to know where their boundaries are and that if they cross it, there WILL be consequences. Children crave security so much that they will even provoke you to discipline them just for the attention. They crave it and if you don't give it to them, they will keep pushing you for it. Learning through rewards is always more effective than learning through pain.

It is however also essential to avoid being over controlling. Let your kids make mistakes, it builds character and strength. If you try to make them perfect, it will only lead to disappointment and worthiness issues.

Your security in yourself is also a very important factor. If you are insecure and go to all kinds of extremes to find acceptance, like putting others down, children pick up on that and feel unsafe. They'll probably become insecure themselves.

Your other big job as a conscious parent is to pass that consciousness on to your children and be a constant example of that. When adults behave consciously, children will learn to behave consciously too and develop good emotional and social intelligence, which will help them tremendously through the rest of their lives. Learn to share, play nicely, hold hands, walk don't run, stop fighting with your siblings. Children do what you do, not what you say. You need to show the child how to stay in control of emotions, don't get angry or shout at him, stay calm but firm. You need to show constant love toward the child, even during discipline and most of all play with them and enjoy them because this is the way to a child's heart. They remind us how to have fun and not take life so seriously.

Often parents work so hard to give their children the best that they ironically neglect to give them the best - love and attention.

Lastly, never ask children to be responsible for something they cannot control and never make children handle adult issues. They have more than enough time to do all that later, let them enjoy just being kids for as long as possible.

Here are a few pointers to remember in everyday relationships:

People learn much faster through reward than through punishment.

Love does not always win on earth but it does in universal laws.

Always think how an angel would act.

Spiritual people often get confused between acting in love and being submissive. Act in love but stand up for what you believe in.

Sometimes it is just a test for you to see if you can keep calm and act in love or if you will be pulled into the illusion and act in ego.

People will jump up and down when you act in love because you are not giving them the control they want.

The only way to get someone to change is to increase their motivation for change.

Fear

Fear is probably human being's biggest emotion to overcome. Most other negative emotions come from a fear of something. Anger comes from fear of not having your needs met or fear of not being in control, amongst various other factors. Jealousy, hatred, resentment, guilt, etc are all fear based. Anger is only a manifestation of someone's insecurities; what they are afraid of. We only act in attack because we feel little and afraid.
We must ask ourselves "what is it that we are so afraid of?" Just remembering who we are, we can overcome all fear.

All fear comes from the fear of dying and of losing the ego, which is perceived as our identity. It is the body's self-preservation program. When your body is at danger of dying, it sends out adrenaline to help you fight harder or run faster. This is all based on living in nature as humans were intended to. Our bodies cannot distinguish if we are being chased by a lion or simply having a fight with our colleague. All it knows is that you are stressed so it creates adrenaline.
Your body is programmed to warn you against any of these things and cannot distinguish what your situation is. If you were in the wild, certain things would be life threatening and your body is programmed to protect you from these things. Adrenaline gives us the power to fight harder, run faster and feel less pain.
Here are a few examples of how our fear mechanism is programmed:

- If we are different in any way we are at danger of being noticed and being noticed can cause one to be killed. Therefore we always try to fit in with the crowd and are scared to be different.
- If something is bigger than you it can kill you so always strive to be the best, strongest, most clever, etc.

- New or unknown may mean death. Therefore don't take risks and explore the unknown. Stay where it is safe.
- Change can equal death. If there is a drought or even a flood, you will probably die. So don't take chances, rather stay with the devil you know than explore the devil you don't.
- Lack equals death. No food means starvation. Therefore indulge and always make sure you have enough. Don't loose anything, hold onto what you have.
- Abundance can mean death just as much as lack can. If you have what someone else wants, they can kill you for it. Don't be rich or poor, just be average and blend in.
- Don't question authority or the way things are done. If you are a threat you will be taken out. Just follow blindly and if you wonder about something keep it to yourself.
- Pain definitely equals death out in the wild with no hospitals or doctors. Avoid pain at all cost. Once again stay safe and don't expose yourself to anything that can cause pain.
- In the wild loneliness can also lead to death. Who will protect you when you are not looking? Whatever you do, make sure you are not alone. Blend in, follow the crowd, do whatever it takes just to not be alone. Human's biggest issue is to be loved and accepted. This once again comes from fear of being an outcast and therefore death.

You can see how past belief systems have created fear today and how our brains associate today's problems with that past way of thinking. If you were in the wild all the above things would definitely be life threatening but in the world we live in today, they cause more self-esteem problems than anything else.

As you can see there is much less to be afraid of these days than in the past when we lived like hunters and gatherers. When we feel the fear, we must not let it override us but rather analyze it and consider if it is justified or not.

Society plays on these fears and everybody buys into it. It is a major tool in advertising and making money. We are taught to fear accidents, extra expenses, and death of ourselves and loved ones. There is insurance for everything, even for the excess payout of your motor vehicle insurance. Insurance for insurance. The media tells us to be fearful of living, dying, getting sick, being too healthy, being too young, and being too old. You name it; they will try and make money off it. Even religions encourage our fear. They teach us to be fearful of God and the devil, of going to hell and not to heaven, of being punished and of being caste out. They too play on your fear to get money. They play on guilt, limit your freedom, and make you scared of not fitting in or being accepted, all in the name of God.

Ever heard the saying "There is nothing to fear but fear itself"? This is very true. Fear is part of the illusion and the only thing to fear is being pulled into it. Here is a nice way of remembering just that.
F-false
E-evidence
A-appearing
R-real

Fear is the illusion, only love is real. Love dissolves fear and you cannot be afraid when you are feeling love. Identify it as that and challenge your fear's right to control your reality. You are stronger than your fears. Separate yourself from them and thereby you are not identifying with them.
Remember that you are a part of the light and light always overcomes darkness. Darkness is not light's opposing force; it is merely the absence of light. They are not equals. Light will shine through darkness, but darkness

cannot go through light. Fear is the only thing preventing us from finding the light because when we do find it, the fear will be illuminated and therefore eliminated.
God is the light and is always with you, all you have to do is step into the light (consciousness) because being in the light you can never be in the absence of light (the illusion). There can never be fear if there is peace, just step into the light (remember peace).

The light / consciousness is the remembering that everything happens for a reason, and the peace that comes from knowing that there is no darkness. If you know the truth, you cannot have fear. If you have an understanding of how things work, everything happens for a reason and in sequence, how can you ever fear something if you know it is exactly as it should be. You know there is nothing wrong. Something is never wrong, it is always the way it should be.

It is about remembering who you are and that you are invincible and indestructible.
Fear should be afraid of you! If you are scared of anything that means that It is in charge. All you have to do is be in charge, and then it will be scared of you.
For example: If you are afraid of a dog it will probably bite you, but if you tell it to sit or run towards it, it will yelp and run away. You can only be scared of something if you decide that it is stronger than you and then give it the power to be that. Face your fears because suppressing them only makes them stronger and they will continue coming up to haunt you. The same goes for panic attacks. That is the fear grabbing hold of you and getting overwhelmed by it. Take your power back. Challenge the fear to come. This way you are already stronger than it and it won't return.

Anger

As discussed earlier, anger is a side effect of fear. When our expectations are not met, we get angry because we

fear not being in control. We expect things to be a certain way as it makes us feel in control and when our beliefs get challenged we become afraid because that is our security.
When someone hurts us, it's the same thing. Our expectation of their actions is different to the action taken. Remember that nobody can hurt us, we choose whether to feel hurt or not to feel hurt.

Guilt

A feeling of unworthiness, inadequacy, insecurity and unfulfillment is most of the time due to guilt. There are so many things we are taught to feel guilty about - committing a "sin", hurting others (willingly or unwillingly), being weak in situations where "we should have been strong", actions taken in fear, anger or self protection, actions not taken, etc. These things happen all the time and they teach us about ourselves. There is nothing to feel guilty about, it was all meant to happen. Each day is a new day. A new day to start over without the baggage of the past. If you keep carrying the past with you, you can never move away from it.

Guilt is normally fear of not being good enough.
You never have to earn love, acceptance and worthiness, you already are that. Just accept it and own it. God's love is available freely all around you, just let yourself feel it.

Forgiveness

Sometimes it is difficult to forgive because we feel that we are just giving up without justice being served. We want the other to feel the pain they made us feel. It is important to remind ourselves that everything happens for a reason and that it is all pre contracted to learn what we need to. Reminding ourselves of this makes it a little easier to take what we have gained from the experience and use it in a constructive way.
It is easy to fall into the trap of blaming others for our mistakes and set backs but we need to take responsibility for our fears and challenge them. Nobody can do that for

us, they can only bring our fears into the light so that we can examine them and face them. So when we feel anger, we should ideally see it as an opportunity to examine our fears.

The limitations of fear

Fear is one of the most if not the most limiting factor in many people's lives. If it wasn't for fear we would probably dare a lot more, explore, take chances, embrace changes and grab opportunities. We put ourselves in a safety box where we feel safe because we know what's around every corner. Sometimes we even find ourselves in a position where we are bored and stifled in our safety zones but still refuse to explore beyond it for fear of what we may find. Most people spend their entire lives only dreaming about what may be waiting for them but yet never getting there because they are too afraid to change and explore.

Being in a box you will never know the truth. You will only know what other people tell you - the view from their box. The first step to finding that you are in a box of limitations is to wonder if there is anything more to life. As soon as you do this you will automatically start looking for a way out. Our beliefs and fears try to keep us in the box but once we question them, we can be free.

When somebody questions our fears or beliefs, we often get defensive because they are threatening our box, which is our safety zone. This is another way of recognizing them. If something triggers a reaction from you, ask yourself why. What fear or belief is making you defend it?

Knowing vs. believing

It is easy to confuse believing with knowing and stand up for a belief as we would for something we know to be a certain way. The difference between knowing and believing is that knowing comes from a deep, core place inside us that becomes alert when recognizing the truth. Believing comes from experiences or perspectives of other people. Beliefs are based on the illusion or box that we are in and knowing comes from experiencing the outside of the box.

You will only know you are on the outside of the box when you compare yourself to other people and see how you used to be.

Beliefs come from fears. We try to protect ourselves with beliefs; it is the part of the human program that preserves us as we discussed earlier. We create beliefs from past experiences so that we recognize the same pattern that led us to pain last time and avoid it or fight it when it threatens us again.

Knowing comes from the light. There is no fear or protective mechanism involved, there is no need to defend it because you can see that it is not worth arguing with ignorance.

Having our beliefs questioned is the scariest thing a person trapped in their beliefs can experience. Most people even have a safety nest of beliefs protecting and reinforcing their main beliefs. The fact that everything is love does not require you to believe, it only requires you to accept. It is possible for you to deny facts but still that doesn't change them.

The bottom line is that knowing frees us, and beliefs imprison us.

A common belief is that doubt and knowing are opposites but we need to doubt our beliefs in order to find knowing. Doubt your belief in limitations, lack, fear and unworthiness. Doubt all negativity and destroy the beliefs they are based on, just make sure to do this in a positive way.

So instead of asking, "Why can't I afford that thing?" ask, "How can I afford it?" These two questions can send you on entirely different quests. The first reinforces your belief that you can't afford it and the second destroys that belief.

Fear vs. self-preservation

It is common to think that fear is the thing that protects us from hurting ourselves. If it wasn't for fear, we would get up to all kinds of crazy things like jumping off buildings and running in front of cars. Fear, however is different to self preservation. We do not need fear to preserve our bodies and know what is dangerous; we need common sense for that. Common sense can tell you it is not going to be beneficial.

We all will die one day so stop fearing it and thereby wasting energy on worrying about it and fearing it. If you can eliminate your fear of dying by believing that your date to die is destined then you can live a free life and have no fear. You won't have a fear of doing anything because you will die on a certain day whether you are bungi jumping or sitting on the couch. This does not mean that you can ignore your common sense, you can still get seriously hurt, you just won't die.

Worry

Worrying is another form of fear that can easily be avoided. Think for a second if worrying about something has ever changed anything about the situation. Probably not, huh? Often we find ourselves worrying to death about something and in the end everything turns out to be fine or if not, there is nothing our worrying did to fix it. Things never turn out the way we anticipate them and worrying about it only gives us insomnia, high blood pressure and lots of other things to worry about. As difficult as it is not to worry about our problems and potential problems, it is to our best advantage to not let it get us down or worry about it. When we are stressed and worried, we cannot think straight either so there is even less chance of us finding a solution.

This doesn't mean we must ignore our problems. Ignoring our problems won't solve anything, but neither will worrying. That is where meditation comes in. It gives us an open mind for solutions to come in. As long as we are busy worrying, our minds are too busy and there is no space for a solution to enter.

There are several things you can implement in your life to avoid things that can cause worry:
Don't do anything that can lead to you worrying about it. Always be honest and do the right thing so that you have a clear conscience.
Don't create situations that put you under unnecessary pressure, they will only lead you to worrying about them. Debt, unnecessary spending, unrealistic work deadlines, and bad time management are just a few examples.
Always remember that you have a choice on how to act. Your actions or reactions can change everything.
Don't fall into the trap of letting fear be your motivation and don't let promises be your motivation either.

The more we worry about something, the more we are paying attention to our fears and giving them more energy so they can grow until eventually they are all we know. Our fears become our reality because they are all we see. If you focus on your fear, you are focusing on the illusion and cannot see reality.

Freedom

Freedom is like pregnancy, just like being either pregnant or not, you either are free or you are not. You cannot be partially free. The only way to be completely free is to let go of all our fears and inhibitions. Only this allows us to experience life to the fullest.
Fear is the main illusion that keeps us from knowing the truth. Christians would say "Fear is the main thing Satan uses to keep us from God's blessings". Why let it limit you, be free.
Acceptance brings freedom.

Healing power

Every one of us has the ability to heal ourselves and others.
The body is just a space suite and illness is just an illusion. We are perfect in every way and the body only reflects what is going on in the mind, i.e. beliefs, masks, labels, etc.
As we discussed earlier, most physical illnesses are due to stored emotions and once we release those, the healing can begin.
We are like the ray from the sun shining our light and warmth (love) on everyone. That is how the healing power works. You have to tap into the greater power, then visualize it and feel it work. Don't make it work. It does not come from you but rather through you.

Here is an energy technique to assisting healing:
Lay your hands on the area that is in need of healing. Take deep breaths and imagine sweeping energy from your feet up to your head with the in breath. With the out breath sweep the energy from your head, through your arms and into your hands. Focus on a feeling of love whilst doing this and don't try and heal anything, just believe it has already happened. In some cases it needs to be done for extended periods of time and several sessions and in other cases, 5 minutes is sufficient.
Sound too simple, doesn't it? This is just a very brief explanation but if you are really interested, you can do a course in "Quantum touch".

When people won't heal

Sometimes illness is a karmic thing and it will not go away until a certain lesson is learned. Sometimes it is a destiny thing and the person has chosen to experience a certain illness in this life.
Sometimes people are not ready to release the emotions they are holding onto and the illness will not shift until they are ready. They may ask to be healed and insist that

they are ready but in actual fact they just want the symptom to go away without doing anything for it. Hence, there are so many symptom suppressants on the market. Someone may ask for physical healing but at the same time if they were healed physically, the threat that brings to their belief systems may be far scarier than the physical expression of it. Therefore they are merely asking for a physical symptom or the expression of the emotion to go away and not for healing.

Remember that you are not the healer. Every person is their own healer. You are just the assister. Therefore you cannot take credit when someone is healed and you cannot take blame if they are not. You may ask “what is the point of attempting to assist someone heal then?” Sometimes people are ready to heal but someone needs to be there to help them release the emotions or lift their physical vibration to a level where healing can happen. It is easier to do it with someone’s help than to do it alone.

Using Energy

Apart from manifesting, there is a lot one can do with energy.
A good way to create consciousness around you when you are in a situation or problem is to create an energy pyramid around you. Don't make it complicated, you just need to imagine it and it will be. Put love at the top and you can anchor the corners with joy, harmony, peace, gratitude, happiness, light or any of these positive consciousness aspects. Check out the power of healing pyramids on the internet to get a good idea of the power pyramids have.
You can also create spheres around doors or around yourself for protection or peace or anything for that matter.

While we are discussing energy I feel the need to clarify "energy exchange". This is something new age people are very familiar with but are often very confused about. It is commonly known that energy exchange happens in every situation between people all the time but the type of energy exchange we are discussing here is where some kind of payment is given in exchange for healing. "Natural Healers" believe that for every "healing" they do, the person receiving the "healing" has to pay for it in some way otherwise the "healer" takes on their karma or the illness and the person wanting healing will not be healed. Payment does not always have to happen with money, it can be done with services or anything that is agreed upon by both parties.
I'm all for being paid for your time and effort when doing "healing" but I don't believe that that person's illness or karma will be transferred to the practitioner if there is no payment. The person receiving the "healing" may not appreciate the effort as much if they are not paying for it so it certainly adds value to the session and in that way it might influence the effectiveness of the session but love

and healing belongs to the universe, not to us personally so we cannot charge for "giving healing" as such.
I have a problem with people offering "to do some healing" for someone and then asking for something in exchange afterwards. The "payment" should be agreed upon first and if the "healing" is offered, not asked for; a payment should not be expected.

Diet

Many people believe that diet has a huge influence on being conscious. It is commonly believed that one has to firstly, be vegetarian and secondly, follow a healthy lifestyle in order to be conscious.

It is a fact that the body functions better on healthy food than on junk food and that your health is a direct effect of what you put in your mouth.

One of the first steps to becoming conscious is to start questioning things and become aware of things around you and this includes your diet and how food affects you.

Junk food makes our minds dull, makes us feel groggy, affects our moods and lowers our level of general awareness. Meat especially is full of toxins, antibiotics, steroids and many other mind and mood altering substances.

Although I do believe in following a healthy lifestyle, I don't believe that being healthy or being vegetarian are prerequisites to becoming conscious. The body is after all an illusion and so is the food, it affects the mind, which is also an illusion but it cannot affect the soul. If your journey in this life involves becoming conscious, there is nothing that can stop that process from happening, least of all your diet.

Another problem I have seen in people who are vegetarian for "spiritual" reasons is the judgment on others that comes with it. Judging others and making yourself superior is spiritual arrogance and defeats the whole object.

Universal laws

Consciousness is a set of universal laws. How things work. These laws never change. So when we learn how to control our lives we are not somehow asking for or getting special favors. We are simply learning how to use these laws to our advantage, as God wants us to. Perfect harmony is the nature of God and consciousness so if we flow with it, we experience harmony. If you go against it, you deny it.
Here are some of the main universal laws:

- What you believe you will create
- You have free will to live in consciousness or unconsciousness
- You can have anything you want but if it interferes with or harms others, there are consequences.
- Every action has a self-created consequence.
- Everything is one and everything that is said, done and thought, affects everything around us.
- Everything is made up of vibrating energy and every thing has its own vibrational frequency.
- Every action has a reaction or consequence
- Negative energies attract negative energies and positive energies attract positive energies.
- Every person will receive a series of problems (Tests) for the purpose of becoming conscious.

The Ten Commandments are more guidelines to living consciously. Follow the laws and life becomes easier, it's as simple as that.

I'm not going to elaborate too much on Universal laws as specifics, as there are many books on the market that will do just that.

Not getting it right

When we experience things like illness, lack, failure, etc, despite trying to live consciously, it is easy to become angry and resentful at ourselves for not getting the consciousness thing right. This only brings about more unconsciousness so the best thing to do is to thank the experience and continue on.

Although consciousness may deprive us of enjoying life's pleasures as when we were in ignorance, it brings a great peace. It brings a knowing that we were right, that there is more to life, there is something better out there and that we are on a mission with a purpose. It helps us deal with the longing and yearning better.

It is not about getting it right all the time and being the example of a perfect human being. We are still humans having human experiences and as long as we try and be conscious about it, we are winning. The trick that we are mostly trying to achieve is to avoid lingering on old emotions and to work through them as quickly as possible. Often we also get given certain experiences to be able to help others go through that same experience.

If you are trying to live in consciousness and don't see results straight away, don't loose faith in your abilities. Just keep seeing and clearing out all your worthiness issues. Its not about having faith in yourself, it's about having faith in God and you are a part of that so you automatically, without even trying, have access to the abilities and abundance.

Never allow yourself to fall into guilt when it proves to be difficult to stay in consciousness. Just keep trying. Simply keep building your faith in what is real.

When you are living the spiritual path it is easy to fall into the trap of pretending that you are always happy, successful, etc even when you are not. There is a fine line between keeping a positive attitude and deceiving others with false pretenses. It is ok to admit when you are not

100 percent and it does not make you a failure, you are still human having a human experience.
When you fall into the illusion don't condemn yourself or feel guilty. Simply recognize that you are not at peace and then choose to be at peace again.
God's will for you is only total peace and joy so if you are not experiencing that, it is only because you are denying it for yourself. This creates a feeling of aloneness, yet you can never be alone because you are one with God and this peace and happiness. It is only the fear of being alone that keeps you in the illusion of aloneness.

www.ingramcontent.com/pod-product-compliance
Ingram Content Group UK Ltd.
Pitfield, Milton Keynes, MK11 3LW, UK
UKHW041847190726
13854UKWH00002B/766